# HEAR MARA'S VOICE

# Hear Mara's Voice

By Milka Djakovich Bamond
Author/Translator

# Prologue

$\mathcal{I}$ am the only living child of Ilija Opsenica and Mara Vrcelj. Being the first and only American -born child of my family on the one hand was a miracle that offered me a better life than my family had, but on the other hand, it separated me from the rest of my kin, all of whom remained in Europe. Never having the opportunity to meet or to know my grandparents, aunts, uncles, or cousins left a huge void in my life.

Therefore I relied exclusively on Mama's tales of her life and the lives of her relatives. My sense of being disconnected was especially painful in my early years as I observed families gathered together. Often times I resented those people.

Recalling exactly at what point in my childhood it was that my brain began to store all the details of mama's life's story would be difficult. As early as age two, I have recalled certain events that profoundly impacted on my memory. However, recall of dialogue came later—perhaps in my fourth year.

To gain Mama's attention, I plied her with questions relentlessly. I invented a game in which I would give myself a made up name—such as Mrs. Nadich—and Mama would be named Mrs. Pekich. Pekich and Nadich were Serbian names I probably heard at some point in my earlier years. From birth to about my third year, English was a foreign language to Mama and me. Throughout our countless conversations spanning decades, and despite our becoming bi-lingual, Serbian was exclusively spoken between us. The task of translating into English required constant attention to Mama's vernacular which was influenced by a life of illiterate peasantry in a region devoid of schools or churches. The Serbian dictionary's pages were dog-eared and a testament to some learned man's efforts.

Engaging Mrs. Pekich in conversation, I would ask her about a fictional little girl in Europe. Did she like this little girl? Was she good? Was she smart? What did she look like? And more inquiries along those lines. Mrs. Pekich (Mama), would not have a great deal of patience for such prattle—so oftentimes I would ask her to just say, "Aha" as I continued to supply the dialogue for the two of us. As time passed Mama began to tell me about that little girl in Europe, sometimes ending the story abruptly—angrily—and once she even cried. That almost ended the playacting for me. However, I began to realize that it was my mother's life's story that was being revealed to me.

And so it began. Over and over I asked her to "tell me again," and she, over and over, told me more and more—indelibly filling my mind. Everything—every detail, every emotion, every event that she talked about—became a part of me. She talked while I listened throughout her lifetime, and now, late into my own, I need to tell her story—for my children, grandchildren, and now you too, dear readers.

Hear Mara's story—in her own voice, if you will. It is strong, clear, brassy, defiant, cruel, judgmental, and boastful, yet honest, brave, proud, and most of all humble, as she spoke to God daily. Come now—meet her.

*"Telling and retelling my life's story to my daughter Milka, my only child, has finally, according to her, become something people might be interested in reading. Admittedly, my journey through life has alternately been bizarre, maddening, depressing, and even inspiring to me. See what you think."*

# *Chapter 1*

My journey began on May 3, 1893, in a small, remote village named Blata in the Kingdom of Alexander I, Monarch of Serbia, Croatia, and Slovenia. Blata means mud. We slogged in mud, which was a result of melting snow of the surrounding mountains. Because of the formation of clay and rock in our valley, drainage was poor, and puddles were a constant.

At the time Europe's ever-changing borders were responsible for much confusion in what constituted one's homeland.

My people, insofar as I can ascertain, are a blend of Serbian, Croatian, and Austrian. The other very real possibilities are Turk, Mongol, and wandering unidentified bands of marauders marching through much of the territory that eons later became Yugoslavia.

Tracing one's roots could be full of obstacles—fanciful dramas often told and retold by great-grandfathers, grandfathers, fathers, uncles, and friends—all claiming glory days in the service of winning armies, spectacular defeats of the enemy, and triumphant conquests of lands. Yet the truths were and still are shrouded in faint memories of what really happened. Besides the victors wrote much of any country's history.

Learning that I was probably the product of much mixing of bloods throughout the centuries of conflict in that part of the world has led me to feel comfortable in the midst of any and all people declaring themselves Serbians, Croatians, Slovenians, Orthodox, Catholic, or Muslim and others. I carry within me the elements of sisterhood to people of all the world's races and religions. Teaching these important principles to my child and grandchildren has enhanced their lives, I know.

# Chapter 2

For the first five years or so of my life, I lived with my parents and siblings, two sisters and five brothers. Our shelter could hardly be referred to as a house, in part because of its diminutive size. The crudely made walls were of roughly hewn, heavy boards and a great deal of mud plastered between the cracks. The roof was made of straw treated with pitch. The dirt floor was packed to the hardness of stone. One room was divided by heavy, black, thickly woven wool panels that separated the parents' sleeping area from the children's sleeping area, leaving the largest area with an oven and fireplace. The fireplace with its hanging cooking pots provided warmth in cold winter months—some warmth, but not much.

My goodness, at this moment, in my mind, I see the craziness of mealtime at my parents' home. It was customary to put the food in one huge wooden bowl in the center of the table. No individual place settings and no silverware. So just imagine that bowl as it meets the tabletop—and suddenly there is an explosion of wooden spoons attacking the food. You see, as soon as you were old enough to join this kind of feeding frenzy, you were given your own wooden spoon. You kept it hidden somewhere or tucked into your waistband. Lose your spoon, and you lose some meals. Looking back this really embarrasses me. Not until I came to America did I know how other people behaved at mealtime.

No, actually, that is not true. My travels through Austria, Germany, and finally France as I embarked on my journey to America gave me my first lessons of life as practiced in other lands.

Please don't think that all mealtimes were that wild. Soup required individual bowls, as did other liquid foods. Solid, hearty concoctions were the most common.

Somewhere around the fifth year of my life, my father was killed by a bear. Bears and wolves were a constant threat year round. In the months of winter, bears were more dangerous to humans and livestock. As horrible as the circumstances of his death were, I remember feeling relief. My father, Juran, was not a kind man.

In my young life, I had viewed many a dead person. There was nothing fearful about it, unless it was a child, then I began to worry about my own death.

My father's body was wrapped in white linen from head to toe, no part of him showing. There was a great deal of discussion among family and friends that my father had been careless. He had ventured out to relieve himself without his gun, and he was found without his knife as well. Speculation as to whether he was drunk or not kept the opinions and theories going for a long time.

My mother was surrounded by her mother and by her sisters for a day or so. Then it was business as usual. I was certain Juran was not missed.

# Chapter 3

Whispers, whispers—I had become aware of them. Instinctively an overwhelming sense of uneasiness was enveloping me. Whenever I was within hearing range of my mother, Aunt Mileva, and some of my older siblings, the whispers turned into nervous, meaningless banter. Young minds, still uncluttered by the less-than-noble deeds and thoughts of adults, can amazingly assimilate, analyze, and reach reasonable conclusions. To prove it test your own children or grandchildren. Ask them about something you believe they are too young to understand. A child's amazingly deductive mind will astound you. They see right to the heart of a situation. We can and should learn from them.

The whispers were heralding my pending immediate future. Some days passed, and the whispers had subsided, now being replaced with uncomfortable glances. Something was about to happen. Without any reservation I was certain that all of this strange behavior had something to do with me.

On a cold, rainy Sunday afternoon an eerie joviality, obviously forced, awkwardly hung in the air. I had not failed to notice our neighbor Adam's ox hitched to our rickety wagon. Our ox had previously succumbed to old age. Wondering why this should be, I approached the wagon and saw the trunk, the top of which I used as a bed. Also there was a roll of blankets, now thoroughly soaked. "What is this?" I asked myself.

In an unguarded moment, as I mused the strange happenings, I was lifted into the back of the wagon by Adam. By then I too was soaked. The air was frosty—spring felt more like winter. I felt numb.

Adam took the reins as my mother wordlessly clambered up unto the seat next to him. Shivering, I tucked my hands into the underarms of my sweater, trying to keep them warm. The bumpy road jarred me so badly I could not sit up. My feet kept coming out from underneath me; there was no keeping them warm either.

The ruts and humps soon gave birth to a rhythm with me humming along, in my head only, I think. Such flights of fantasy entertained me. Knowing that people's thoughts could not be read guaranteed me endless journeys into mental escapades. Our destination was unknown to me, yet the unease I had felt for some days was now, in my mind, becoming a set in stone feeling of doom. We rumbled on for some time. All the while it continued to rain.

Obviously this trip to wherever we were going was not one conceived in any sort of openness with me. It became evident that I was the reason for this journey. The whispers were about me. I was certain. "Sit up. Look alive, Mara," my mother ordered. "We are here at my sister's house." So what was so important to include my presence at the home of an aunt I had never met?

The open doorway to the little house was filled with a figure of a mammoth man. "Oh, you are here," is all that he said.

He walked to the back of the wagon, poking a finger into my chest. I felt a little pain and pulled back. Looking up into his eyes, I cringed as a new fear joined the already frightening emotions that consumed my mind. From that moment on, my uncle became "that devil" in my personal, silent reference to him. That devil was tall and gaunt. His thick, unkempt beard covered his mouth, concealing the fangs I was certain were there. Huge hands and feet seemed to weigh him down. To me he was a monster. At what point I became aware of my surroundings, I cannot recall. It was my mother's voice that forced me to focus and react in an automatic, unfeeling fashion.

"Mara," she was speaking to me in her sternest, unkindest tone. "You are to stay here with your Aunt Danila and her husband Anton. This is your new home; do not return to me. I don't want to have any more trouble with you. My sister has no children; now she has you."

Without so much as a glance in my direction she hurried out the door. Tears were unknown to me. My mother never allowed such a display of weakness, as she called it. However, my eyelids were burning. I often wondered where the tears went.

I have vivid memories from the time of my separation from my family. I believe that my mother was possibly twenty-eight years old. Her face was stony hard, and her forehead deeply furrowed. She had a thin-lipped mouth; small, black, piercing eyes; and a compact, muscular body. It was her walk that impressed me. Always square-shouldered, with small, brisk steps, arms freely swinging, and eyes focused straight ahead as though seeing something the rest of us were missing. In my young mind, I saw her walk as a personal declaration of freedom and untouchable aloofness. I walk the same way.

My father, Juran, evokes only memories of a cruel, abrasive personality. The details of his physical self escape me. He was a nonperson to me as far back as I am able to recall. In later years, when trying to reconstruct some of the details of being sent away to my aunt, I wondered if his death played any part in my being sent away. I had no way of knowing, yet it disturbed me.

Why did she select me? I was the third-youngest child, already useful and very obedient. My youngest brother, Radan, was mean and very difficult—so like our father. He had already tried to chop off my hand as I picked up wood from the ground, partially severing the first joint of my little finger on my left hand. So why me, while she kept the other seven children?

Not until I was in my seventies did I learn of a theory that could explain the reason I was selected. My daughter, Milka, while telling her friend, Beverly, the circumstances surrounding my mother's decision to send me away, she, Beverly, without a moment's hesitation, said, "The answer seems obvious to me." She reasoned that I was not fathered by my mother's husband. That I was most likely the product of an indiscretion or even a rape. So with her husband's death, she could rid herself of the constant unhappy reminder of my origin. So fact or fiction, that analysis seems logical to me. Thank you, Beverly.

# Chapter 4

*A*unt Danila was not visible to me, not from the first moment of my arrival, nor for the following several days. My uncle had put my trunk in a corner of a very small, windowless space. Then he slung one of the still-wet blankets over the trunk

"That should be dry by tomorrow. If not, I'll dry it by the fire. Now go to sleep," he ordered. It was still daylight, but I pretended to be sleepy.

Later while standing in the doorway of my space, my uncle noticed that I had not gone to sleep as he had ordered me to do. He cleared his throat loudly and said, "It is too early to sleep, so if you are hungry, find yourself something on the table."

He walked to my trunk and touched the damp blanket. "It can't dry out in here; I'll lay it right next to the fireplace, and oh yes, I already told you that. Your fool mother, sister to my dim-witted wife, should have protected your blankets and you from the rain. She must have at her disposal some oiled fabric; we all do. Well anyway, I'll get a pallet for you. It's in the barn."

In his absence I found some cold beans, dried out from repeated reheating, and some bread, equally dry and really hard. It would have been nice to dip the bread into some kind of liquid. Still, it was something.

My uncle returned and slung a pallet onto the floor as it was much too large for the top of my trunk. The smell of the pallet was choking. The musty smell of the long ago broken down, crushed straw was irritating to my nose and throat. My eyes burned. The pallets at home, at least, were sweet smelling, with a sturdy white fabric covering them. My mother religiously attended to such things. Our bedding was frequently aired in the sun and tossed about to loosen the straw, preventing it from compacting into a solid, hard, smelly mass of prickly slivers poking through the worn and soiled fabric covering it—such as the one I was just gifted with.

No explanations were necessary. I never questioned anything my mother or other adults said or did. However, I slept on the dirt floor that night. Other nights I slept on the top of the trunk without a pallet. In really cold weather, the trunk's top was a blessing, even though, as I grew, I could no longer stretch out. That first night sleep eluded me—I felt unsafe, especially when I could hear my uncle mumbling.

Finally, my Aunt Danila presented herself. As I recall she came in the door at what I imagine was noon time or thereabouts. I was in my space at the time. The first words out of her mouth were, "Where is she?"

"Where do you think?" my uncle countered. "She sits uselessly on the floor in there. She will have to learn, the sooner the better, that there is work to be done."

Danila screamed out, "Come out here!"

I decided beforehand that I would not be fearful of her, and it proved to be so. She looked very fierce, yet the hesitation as she spoke, the glances at her husband, signaled to me a fear of her own. In later years I began to understand her escape into alcohol. The jail where she spent a good bit of her time was a safer place than her home—away from that devil.

The irony of the presence of a jail when the village had no school or church always puzzled me from the start. It was the same in my village. It was a three-day trek to the nearest church. Where a school might have been, I never found out.

Scanning her body quickly, for I could not bear to look at her for long, I saw a plumpish, stoop-shouldered figure somewhat precariously planted atop a pair of shaky, very hairy legs, exposed by her tattered skirt. Bruises and sores were visible on her legs despite all that hair. She had feet, oversized for her body, with thickly calloused soles and unkempt toenails that were cracked and stained.

She presented a very unappealing first impression. Her babushka was loosely tied, slipping to one side of her head and exposing disheveled hair. There was some resemblance to my mother and her other sisters, but at least they were clean. How odd, I thought, that her hair was in such a state.

All the village women cared for their hair. Protection from the sun and dust was important to keeping the hair shiny and healthy. Babushkas were ever present when the women worked in the fields. Washing one's hair was a major project. Drying it was even more time consuming in front of the fireplace in the winter. Shampoos were infrequent. Yet the hair was always groomed. Many styles of braids, coils, and buns were constantly the subject of what we in America called "girl talk."

Poor Aunt Danila never embraced the idea of improving her appearance.

Poor, hapless, lost soul that she was, Danila struggled to maintain her sobriety. Drink-free periods were so short in duration. Just about the time that I was hopeful that she had overcome her habit, she would succumb again. I hated her for it. Each succeeding episode eroded any feelings I could have had for her. Not that she was motherly in any way, neither was my mother, but I believe that instinctively I wanted it, and somewhere in my mind I was demanding it even though I didn't really know how a mother should behave toward a child.

During one of the infrequent periods of sobriety, my aunt exhibited a flash of interest in me. As young as I was, I concluded that she was trying to be protective of me. Often she cursed my uncle for looking my way.

"You, animal, can't you see she is a mere child?"

His eyes were penetrating, fearsome, sending a numbing chill throughout my body.

"Keep clear of him; he could do you great harm," she warned in a hoarse whisper one night as she knelt beside the trunk I slept upon. It was one of the very few times that she touched me. Stroking my cheek with her work-hardened fingers, she revealed a softer side of herself. Even without my aunt's words of warning, I was more than a little apprehensive of what he might do to me. I developed an ever-present awareness of his whereabouts.

Not having anyone to turn to, I became completely dependent on my own resources of defense. My aunt, although I felt somewhat safer when she was within sight, was no match for her husband. His cursing was often accompanied by physical abuse, which kept her cowering and ineffective as my protector. Believe it or not, even at that point in my life, I felt that I was stronger than my aunt.

My determination to protect myself from him helped me formulate some games within my head. A rusty knife, found in the barn, was to be my weapon of defense. When I used coarse sand to clean the knife, the rust fell away, revealing a blade so jagged and thin I could see it was useless as a weapon. So I went about finding hardened, dry, pointed pieces of wood.

Soon I had a cache hidden here and there. I thought those were deadly weapons.

Praying I would never have to use the weapons, I devised other methods of self-defense. Sneaking out of the house and hiding in the hay was okay, except in the extreme cold of winter. More than once he tried to find me in the hay, muttering, "Just wait, little girl, I will get you." What he meant, I could not possibly understand. As the months and years passed, the state of fear I lived in was making me ill. If only there had been just one person I could ask to take me away.

# Chapter 5

*E*ven when in the midst of the village children, I always
felt as an outsider. The circumstances of my life with the
turmoil in my aunt and uncle's home made me feel ashamed. So
I kept to myself most of the time.

Loving nature as I did, I'd venture into explorations of ant
hills and animal burrows, looking for all kinds of surprises,
even under rocks and in pools of water. I always kept an eye
out for anyone who might observe me.

At the edge of the forest, near an open field, a good distance
from my home was a tiny house surrounded by cherry trees
which for a long time fascinated me. An elderly woman who
lived at the house waved at me whenever I happened to be in
that area. Actually, often I went out of my way just to catch a
glimpse of that hand greeting me.

One day I ventured closer as she called out to me, "My little
soul, come here." She led me into her kitchen, saying, "Eat, eat,
dear little soul, you are empty, I know." Not for long; I felt like

a cow's udder past milking time. Her cow's milk incidentally was sweeter than any other. Just when she mentioned her name was Tina, I can't remember.

Now I know that milk was sweetened by the love she lavished on me. *Oh, life, oh, life*—how much of it I let slip by. Let me tell you, belated tears of regret are better than none.

Looking back more than seventy-five years, the pain in that little "soul" draws tears. If only—if only—she had been my mother or my aunt. "If only" are often lamented words that change nothing. Any opportunity for a close attachment to develop was killed by my distrust and fear, as they overrode my longing for more. Why would this woman offer me freshly baked bread and a cup of milk, just extracted from her cow? The near-delirious savoring of food, touch, and conversation only filled me with guilt.

For almost a year we continued to meet cautiously. We both understood that there could be some unpleasant re-percussions. Nothing about this was ever said by either one of us, but as time passed, we seemed to care less if we ever were found out.

Most of the time, in good weather we sat on a bench at the rear of her home, out of sight. Often she put her arm around my shoulders, and I would squirm away. Stroking my hair, sometimes braiding it was a touch I craved, and I would sit still for that. Sometimes the silence was better than anything we could have said. I was trusting her bit by bit, yet the gnawing question was, why was she so kind to me?

Looking deep into her eyes was the real test of my trust. She would hold my gaze until I looked away. Her eyes were a soft brown, set wide apart in a broad face. Smiling lips revealed strong, squarish teeth. Her face was fair, sagging a bit here and there. What I could see of her hair under the babushka was snowy white. Her hands, I noticed, were soft.

She no longer toiled in the fields. She spoke of a brother who plowed and planted her plot of ground. Once in a while I saw him helping her. Her one lonely cow grazed in an emerald-green field—probably the most contented cow in the entire village.

"Angel" or "little soul" were her pet names for me. She was the only one who had such sweet names for me. Tina had become a good listener. She asked one particular question: Did I ever amuse myself by imagining secret friends—be they human or animal?,

I happily replied: "Oh yes, oh yes, all the time I imagine faces of people and animals." How could she have known?

"How so? Tell me all about it," Tina urged. Having become somewhat more comfortable with her, I felt safe in telling her about my secret game.

"Well, I see faces in everything. I look closely at anything, trying to find the faces, and sometimes a whole picture appears of houses and things like that. I get really excited when a wind stirs up the dead leaves and twigs in the forest. My eyes can find such beautiful shapes of all kinds, but faces are the best."

Overhead clouds in their constant movement provided an endless source of shapes, big faces and small. Clouds frightened me when there was a storm; I was afraid of seeing mean, evil faces. Once, in the midst of revealing all my imaginings, I threw myself on the ground and placed my ear to the grass.

I turned to Tina and said, "Listen, Tina, like I do. Lie down with me and you will hear the spirit of the earth." Right then an ant tried to get into my ear.

"See, the earth is alive with all kinds of creatures—it is singing with joy. Ants are fascinating to me. I never knowingly step on one. When I milk our cow, I pour a little of the milk around their hills. Why should ants not drink milk? Ants have taught me many a lesson. Some ant must be the commander of the moving lines of workers. They explore all around looking for food, then contact their comrades. Soon more ants arrive; each one knows his job, like me, I know my job—my place in my own hill. Not too different than people, you know."

Tina awakened in me an even greater awareness of my senses. How she did that I can't be sure. In looking back I remember her gentle way of pointing out to me the beauties of nature I had not yet become aware of.

She would tell me of her own experiences as a child, the joyful memories that fed her soul in her adult life.

Through her I began to develop my awareness of everything around me. For example, when I was with her, I became aware of the passion that descended upon me with the fragrance of fresh-baked bread. I always looked forward to a warm chunk of her bread, gobbling it up and wanting more. Tina's story about the little grain of wheat, how it grew, becoming a plant, finally milled into flour, and its crowning glory in becoming a loaf of bread thrilled me. To this day the fragrance of her bread clings to my mind and nostrils. My own baking efforts keep alive that memory and passion.

Tina also awakened in me a keen awareness of the renewal of life. The sweet smell of a new life, if I happened to be near enough to witness the birth of a lamb or calf, clings to me still, as it did then. Whether it was truly sweet or even offensive, I can't be sure. All I know is that the joyousness of birth and the mother's immediate attention to her offspring filled my heart with awe. I always hoped that scent, of whatever kind, would cling to my clothes and body. Sniffing my long hair, there was always that hope that at least it had been there for a while.

Tina would often tell me about things that I needed to know. She was so skillful in telling me that I never realized her objective till later. I guess she felt if I comprehended too much too soon I would bolt. She carefully wove into a story the event that she said would later change me from a child to a young woman. I had heard whispers about "that time of month" yet never questioned the subject. I didn't have time for nonsense. Carefully I absorbed all she cautioned me about, especially boys. "They," she would say, "are very clever; God made them that way. Boys are not bad, but don't put yourself in some place alone with a boy. He might try to kiss you and touch you in places no one has ever touched you—under your clothes. Never let one talk you into lying down with him. His kisses could make your mind go blank. Under no circumstance allow yourself to start feeling strange things. Listen to the beat of your heart and your breathing, they tell you there is danger. Save yourself for the man you marry, only him."

"Oh, yes," I couldn't wait to say to her, "then the babies come, don't they?" I was not too embarrassed to add that I had seen the farm animals do odd things followed in time by babies.

"Oh, I know," I said to her. Once I heard my grandmother telling my oldest sister to be careful, or she would wind up like one of our cousins. Everyone talked and laughed about her till they found her dead, hanging in the barn.

I asked, "Why is it bad to have a baby before marriage?"

"It just is. Take my word for it. So be watchful, Mara." I knew she was annoyed with me; she called me Mara.

After that I stayed away for a while. Maybe she didn't want to see me anyway. Like a fool I stayed away too long. Tina was buried near the beautiful cherry trees. A small cross marked the spot. I made wreaths of flowers or green leaves and hung them on the cross.

Such a sweet sampling of kindness. I did not fully comprehend the magnitude of my loss when she passed on. Not until I became an old woman, even older than Tina was when she left us. Only in the recent past did I really value all that she did for me. Sure, it was enjoyable to visit her, to bask in the sunshine of her persona, to partake of the food, to listen to her stories and most of all her valuable advice. Oh, her advice saved me a time or two. Tina's counseling served me well throughout my life. Bits and pieces sometimes, but her words were potent. Early on, as I said, the information was tucked away somewhere in my brain.

Amazingly, her words surfaced at much unexpected times. Case in point, when I became aware that a lady friend of mine was having an affair. Tina's well-phrased admonition about such conduct was fresh in my mind, every word.

"Child," she had said, "we are born male or female, we do not get to choose which. However, I say to you, it is easy to be a female, to act like the female animals that we are. So once married, do not think for a moment that some other male is better than your man. Dismiss that thought. Be steadfast in a very important decision to not behave as a female. As I said, that is easy. Instead strive to be a woman. There is a vast difference between the two.

"You will understand someday." Tina's words imprinted in my mind so deeply that I, in my lifetime, was never tempted to stray.

# Chapter 6

Such a beautiful day it was. It had inspired me to complete a piece of embroidery that I was going to attach to a blouse as a decoration.

Tina had tried several times to get me interested in embroidery. I sensed her disappointment; however, she never pressed me about it.

Tina's son traveled about the country. When he brought her gifts from his visits, they were surprises. Her son's name was Pero, a fine looking man, just as mild mannered as his mother. He spent a great deal of time talking to me a time or two, much to my amazement. Children, especially girls, were not paid much attention by adults. Pero made me giggle and smile, nothing silly, you know. It was just so much interesting information about places and things he had seen and done.

Well, anyway, I'd been thinking about Tina so much that I rummaged through some of my belongings to find this forgotten and neglected project. Actually I had put it away most carefully, having rolled it up in an old but clean nightshirt. There it all was, a piece of silk cloth and many strands of soft, beautiful embroidery thread, a few needles, a thimble, and small scissors.

Tears welled up and spilled down my face when I recalled Tina, as it often made me sad at first, then I found comfort in the beautiful memories. The reason I was so resistant to the whole embroidery thing was that embroidery thread such as Tina's was not only scarce in our village but unobtainable from our few peddlers. In addition, the silk cloth was such a luxury and not often seen in our parts. I felt like a thief who might steal away Tina's treasures, gifts her son had given her.

So on this particular day, my spirits were high, buoyed by the pleasant weather and the place I called my own. The trees overhead, the soft grass and bugs aplenty, had transported me into my own heaven. My joy suddenly ended as thoughts of my Aunt Danila recovering from last night's beating jolted me with a shameful guilt. I should have stayed with her.

Instead I escaped to the woods whenever the devil uncle made his own escape to the *birtija,* a saloon—to brag, no doubt. Fortified with alcohol, he could be dangerously out of control. Cautiously I sneaked into the back of the house. Aunt Danila was kneading bread dough, alternating punching and cursing as sweat dripped off her chin.

"Quick, hide. He has been looking for you. I told him I sent you to Mila's house for some poppy seeds."

I hugged her waist in thanks.

# Chapter 7

The show down with my uncle occurred somewhere around my ninth year. The devil uncle caught me during a lapse of watchfulness as I sat under a tree near the edge of the forest. My needlework spread around me had taken my mind off him.

Much to my shock, he threw himself upon me. Swearing and laughing, he pressed ever harder on my entire being. Having the wind knocked out of me left me slow to grasp the seriousness of my lack of defense. A pair of small scissors, still clutched in my hand, had jabbed my leg in the attack. Yet I was able to free my arm, and with a fierce surge of strength, I brought the scissors up into his armpit, breaking apart the scissor blades. My surprise counterattack set off in him a torrent of yelling.

Having rolled off me, he still had a steel-like grip on my right leg. Then, jumping up, he reached for a small fallen tree limb with the obvious intent of striking me. Being a child, I outran him, screaming at the top of my lungs, heading for a neighbor's house. Thinking I would be protected, I was instead greeted by the man of the house with the words, "Ha, here comes the refuse of Anton's house. Get away from here; go to your mother, worthless girl."

I realized then that I was just that—refuse. My own mother had thrown me to these wolves, leaving me marked as a worthless person. I ran to my aunt and uncle's house. Thank God, my aunt was in the house.

"Hide me!" I begged, "Uncle Anton has tried to kill me!"

"What can I do for you, child? He will beat both of us."

Instead, some of his rage had subsided, so it was a half-hearted sort of reprisal of just cursing.

"Keep her out of my sight," he ordered my aunt. "She means to kill me; see this wound so close to my heart?" he bellowed.

There was little jubilation for me, as I realized that now he would be fueled by vengeance. My situation had worsened, as now I was in even more danger.

My little leg wound inflicted by the scissors left a small scar—a constant reminder of the devil uncle. Even before I left my mother's home, I had decided that all men were beastly. Observations within my own family formed my opinion of men. My father, as I remember him before his horrible death, was cruel and brutal to my mother, all my siblings, and of course, me. After his death my brothers, emulating our father, became the new tormentors.

In my young judgment, I saw women as the stronger of the two sexes. It's so simple to beat us, demean us, demand unrealistic hours spent in the fields—but try being a woman, I'd say to myself. Everything falls upon the shoulders of the women. The very survival of the family and the village, was assured by their toughness, their unwillingness to be crushed, no matter what. The men were always rummaging about, looking for food stores hidden and protected by the women. How else would they and their children survive? To me it seemed like a game that the men always lost. It was clear to my young mind that they were stupid, and they were dependent on the very ones they abused, the ones who kept it all bound together. These observations fed my resolve to never trust the male sex.

# *Chapter 8*

*M*ost of the time I was without any foot protection. We did not have shoes as you know them. For special times, if we were lucky, peddlers coming to our village had sandals of such soft, supple leather. The sole was brought up to the sides, fastened with thin, narrow strips of leather in a variety of patterns, then further secured with leather lacing which was also decorative and lent strength and durability to the sandal. The toe of the sandal was upturned, resembling what you might think of a harem dancer's slippers. Of course, that was a Turkish influence, a reminder of the Ottoman Empire that controlled my people's lives for five hundred years.

Bare feet were the rule of the day. Even very young feet developed thickly callused soles and toes. On the cold days of fall and very early spring, the cold ground was painfully unbearable. We hopped from foot to foot, anything to keep the blood moving. Calluses rubbing against near-frozen ground produced friction enough to somewhat build up a bit of heat, at least it felt that way.

An alternative to bare feet in severely cold weather is a method of bundling or wrapping up one's feet in coarsely woven wool fabric coated with animal fat for water proofing. The fabric was strapped to the feet with strips of the same material. Then there were the heavy boots also purchased from the peddlers. Their cost minimized the number of boots a family could purchase. I never had a pair.

Even before I began to live with my aunt and uncle, I was a wood gatherer in our close-by forest. I was a sturdy, energetic child. The main purpose of wood gathering was not the sole reason for entering the forest. If a family had a calf, lamb, or goat, it was tied to a length of rope and dragged along into the forest. The theory was that there might be patches of good grazing here and there.

On cold days the animal was an especially welcomed companion. After all there was that occasional freshly excreted dung to keep one's feet warm. My friends and I made a game of it, making bets which of the animals would be the first to oblige. A scramble to claim the gift of warmth sometimes got a bit rough. Boys were usually the winners, yet there was enough to keep all of us happy for a while.

The gathering of wood provided needed kindling for our stoves and fireplaces. Larger pieces of fallen tree limbs were hauled home by adults. Very little tree cutting was permitted, as forest patrols protected property of "the crown." That is not to say that bribes did not allow for more removal of wood than would be permitted. The men who patrolled had their own needs as well. So I never heard of any punishment to anyone.

However, children, very young children, were sent to the forest on a regular basis. You gathered until you had a bundle practically the size of your body. I was good at it and astounded my aunt and uncle with my capabilities. I tied up the bundles at intervals as I kept gathering, which made a much more compact bundle, easier to handle. I could swing it onto my back in one smooth movement. It hurt, of course, making bruises on my shoulders and back. There was satisfaction, however, in being a useful family member.

# Chapter 9

Two holidays—very major holidays, Easter and Christmas—gave all the families something to look forward to, a respite from the drab drudgery of just trying to stay alive.

Even now I recall my anxiety at I learned that Christmas was approaching. Aunt Danila was so vague about everything, and I was especially concerned about the Christmas candles. String which was made of linen, the best my mother could make, was enclosed within beeswax. A small quantity at a time was warmed carefully near the fire while cupped in her hands. As the substance became somewhat pliable, it would be flattened on the wooden tabletop, the linen string wick carefully placed, hopefully in the center of the wax. Until the wax was rolled up around the wick, you couldn't always tell whether the wick was properly centered. Now it was ready for the final touches, as it was rolled between the palms, giving it a smooth gleaming finish.

Grains of wheat were placed in a bowl and germinated into green grass. The Christmas bowl of beautiful, bright-green, grassy-looking, freshly sprouted wheat was a symbol of the prayed-for bountiful crop in the next year. Our best candle, placed in the center of the wheat grass, further enhanced the expectation of a great bounty.

Candles made by my mother, as I remember them, were perfection. Aunt Danila's efforts produced crude, crooked candles, barely holding together. These were our everyday candles.

As Christmas approached I wondered when Aunt Danila would get around to making the candles. One particular morning, I don't remember exactly what I said, but the response was ugly.

"Make the cursed things yourself!" she screamed. "Candles, who needs them? I might not make them this year. Make them yourself."

Now, in my opinion, this was a serious sin. No candles meant no legitimate Christmas, and Christ would be right back in that dark barn.

My mentioning this pending doom to one of the village children, who in turn told it at their home, started a series of events. Before long my hated uncle got wind of my "spilling the beans," as I learned that phrase in America. He said nothing, but there was something going on; I could feel it. A most astounding change in my uncle, which almost made me less fearful of him, happened early one morning as he went about the business of getting breakfast together.

He abruptly stopped, stooped low, brought his face close to mine, and asked me in a civilized tone, "Would you want some cheese?" For a moment or so, I was speechless. His beard had been clipped quite short, revealing his heretofore concealed mouth. Expecting to see fangs, I saw instead normal teeth—some were crooked or stained, and one side tooth was missing—but regular teeth. My eyelids, I was sure, were glued open.

"Ah yes, please," I choked out the words, as my throat had dried. I was grateful for the milk as it eased down a mouthful of bread. Those huge hands even looked cleaner. Something was going on. Soon I would find out, as my aunt dragged herself to the table. Her head in her hands, elbows leaning on the table, smelling of something unpleasant, she mumbled something about coffee.

My uncle said, "I'll give you coffee right on your miserable, stupid head. It could wash you up—such a stupid, lazy cow. You disgrace me. You are worthless. I'll put you in jail one day, and you will stay there forever. Not one person in this entire village would disagree with me," he yelled.

He yelled some more, then slammed his fist down on the table, knocking Danila's elbows off.

"This year we will honor Christ in a proper manner," he continued. "I plan to ask my uncle Sima to visit us. This house must be cleaned up; you need to look like the other women. What must this child think of us? Before I married you, I was like the other men. But with you I have become something I am ashamed of. Shame, shame, is what you have heaped on me. Cow, Cow!" he kept yelling.

Where to escape? I slid off the bench and crawled under the table.

What followed was brutal. I covered my eyes, yet I heard it all. He beat her, kicked her, and knocked her down; not a sound did she make. I thought she was dead. He stormed out.

She crawled onto the bed, groaning, "Dog, dog, dog, that's what you are."

I slithered outside. Those "normal" teeth almost had me fooled.

Several days passed, details escape me, and my usual mode of shutting it all out was working just fine. However, there was still something afoot. Surprise of surprises, I noticed my uncle selecting a log that would become the Christmas log. Carefully he was chipping away knots and loose bark. When he saw me, he nodded and asked, "Does this make a fine Christmas log? It is fir—it will burn brightly and perfume the house as well."

The first few years that I had lived with them, I didn't realize that my mother provided them Christmas candles. Cousin Radin came to our village, as he had a friend there, and he brought the candles, obviously before the heavy snow fell at Christmastime.

Several days had passed; all was quiet. My aunt, believe it or not, had magically transformed herself into a clean person. The odor was gone, the hair was groomed, and her mouth had been altered—there were missing lower teeth. I never saw them scattered on the floor or anything like that, so I guessed she had swallowed them when my uncle beat her. Bruises on her face were still swollen. I, in my mind, kept saying, "Dog, dog, dog."

All the traditions were closely carried out. Of course, the Christmas log was ready and waiting. Uncle had placed it well away from the fireplace, lest it be mistaken for ordinary firewood. Straw was strewn on the floor of the house. Some piled high, under the table, representing the manger—Christ's birthplace. Days of preparing the traditional foods gave us a feast to look forward to. Much of the somberness of daily living gave way to a spirit of joyfulness.

My aunt and I made candles. Her hands deftly rolled the candles. They looked as good as my mother's. Uncle hung them by their wicks in an easily seen spot. I guessed he was pleased. The prized traditional piglet had been bought from the one villager who had made a business of raising pigs and lambs for holiday celebrations. Uncle Anton had constructed a spit within the fireplace. Slowly, ever so slowly, the piglet would be rotated, as we would take turns doing so, all the time immersing ourselves in the fragrance. From pale pink to a luscious bronze, the piglet's skin would be transformed into something nearly too perfect to carve up and to consume.

Our sole guest was Uncle Anton's uncle Sima. He was duly impressed. It was a rare visit, and I would bet it was his most memorable one.

Danila, the hostess, had prepared all the required foods for the fasting days preceding Christmas. She was quiet with a dignity never before seen by me. I decided then that my mother's ways were cold, often cruel; the pride in herself was very deep, sometimes overdone, so I would venture to say Danila had grown up the same way.

Going to church often was out of the question. Drifts of snow, high as the eves of the house, pretty much kept us captive. Pathways cleared to the barn, outhouse, and whenever possible, to a neighbor's house required back-breaking daily tending. Icicles formed on high tree branches and eaves of the house, often reaching to the ground. They could be dangerous if disturbed. On occasion word would get about that a serious injury, or even death, resulted from falling icicles. Sparkling in the sunlight, beautifully disguised, their potential for lethal danger sometimes deceived a person.

The greatest surprise, and a miracle, I would say, happened right after Christmas. Aunt Danila awkwardly, but warmly, put an arm around my shoulders.

Bending low, she whispered, "I wanted a girl like you, but I lost her."

A lonely tear glistened on the eyelashes of one eye. Not until I married did I learn of my aunt's loss. Just prior to giving birth, Anton had brutally beaten her. A girl child was expelled, dead. She never conceived again.

# Chapter 10

My life was the same as everyone else's. Sometimes I would abruptly stop to count up the many years I had spent with my relatives. My feelings of abandonment continued. Daily I reminded myself that I was not important to my mother and the rest of my siblings. Although I thought of myself as tough, it did sadden me. I couldn't brush it off—it chewed at me. A time or two, I thought of going home and forcing my family to take me back, but then pride would step in as I mentally thumbed my nose at the lot of them. My family came to see me, as they had other kinfolk nearby, so it was always an obligatory, quick in and out at my aunt and uncle's home. My mother never once visited.

Years went by. Seeing my grandmother and younger sister, Sara, arriving in a wagon with my uncle Mitcha set off some questions in my mind immediately. It was not just a drop-in visit; I felt it. Were they coming to discuss marriage? Surely not mine. Of course, it had to be about my Sara.

After a brief, superficial chitchat, my grandmother spoke. "You'll have to marry before Sara. You can't keep her waiting. What's wrong with you? Soon you'll be too old for anyone."

Age eighteen seemed too young to marry; besides, there wasn't anyone in the village that I would even spit on, let alone marry. Such a bunch of mean roughnecks, ready to pounce on any female—human or not. Oh, I'd seen a sample or two of such gang activity. Of course, it was all just in fun, as the old men excused these activities, probably digging into their own recollections of such "fun."

Then Sara spoke to me about it. "Can't you see that you are spoiling everything for me? This is my chance to get away from here. Uncle Mitcha has made the arrangements with the parents of Adam Jokich. They will come to Blata as soon as we tell them you are going to get married. So as soon as you choose someone, they will announce our engagement."

"Who is this Adam anyway?" I asked. "Must be someone I never knew. Besides, you and grandmother coming here must mean that things are further ahead than I imagined. Uncle Mitcha was here not too long ago, spending a lot of time talking to me. Now I know why. He was not too direct, so I didn't have a notion that you were so close to marriage. Who is he?" I asked again.

Sara said, "Adam is from Ogulin. I have not met him yet, but Uncle Mitcha knows his family, and he tells me that Adam is a very nice-looking boy, has gone to school, and has a good trade. He makes wagons with his father and uncles. That sounds good to me, don't you see? Besides, I would marry him if he was old and toothless, just to get out of here," she breathlessly ended.

Marriage was inevitable. My sister Sara was in a hurry to tie the knot. I knew without a doubt that the hurry was not because of Sara's possible pregnancy. My mother watched her girls like a hawk; good thing too, as the village boys were always skulking around. I knew that frenzied look. My own brothers at that certain age—fifteen or so—and had that same look, besides I heard them talk about "getting her." God, why would you make them like that?

Sara was my favorite sister. She was better looking than the rest of us. Built more slightly, she looked less robust, but still strong. Sara had a much softer voice, spoke slowly, and walked like a lazily passing cloud. Oh, I don't mean she was not industrious or willing to work as hard as any female in our family, she was just nicer in a way I can't explain.

This stupid business of having to marry in the order of one's birth was pushing me into a cage.

Before they left, my grandmother Nada pulled me aside and said, "We've been looking about for someone for you to marry. Uncle Mitcha gets around more than the rest of us. There will be a problem though. Danila and Anton are not your parents and are under no obligation to offer a dowry for you. So I will talk to the family and see what we can put together. Combined we will put something together, but it will not be very much.

You have to marry soon, you know that? So look about your own village. There must be someone."

My aunt and uncle were now fully aware of my situation. "You can't put marriage off too long," said Anton. "Besides, you can't be too picky."

Boy, did I know that.

At least three months had dragged by, and with the passing of time, the marriage subject slipped further and further from my mind. Then one Sunday afternoon in May, a couple I'd never seen before presented themselves at our house. I happened to be seated at the table, sorting beans and discarding the bad ones, so I was absorbed in my task. They startled me. The door was open. I thought I heard the sound of shoes at the stoop. Thinking it was my aunt or uncle, I did not look up until I heard a man's voice.

"Greetings," he said. "Are we at the home of Anton Jorich?"

I jumped up, wiping my hands on my soiled apron. "Yes it is; I am his niece, Mara," I said.

Luckily, right about then the absent pair arrived. "Hello, Nikola, what brings you here?" My uncle was jovial and animated as he welcomed them, offering them wine and brandy. Danila eagerly brought out the glasses and a large plate full of pogacha, a flat, delicious bread. I didn't know what to do with myself. Was I supposed to join them? I would have preferred to just walk outside, away from it all. So I sort of edged my way toward the door. No such luck. I was called back.

Anton pointed to a chair and said, "Do sit down, dear Mara. Mr. and Mrs. Opsenica have come to seek your hand in marriage. They have heard all about you. They know you are ready for marriage, as is their son Ilija."

At the sound of that name, my mouth dried up quickly. I didn't say a word. What could I say?

"He is an apprentice with a blacksmith. He will be able to provide for you. That is a very good trade, as you know. We will give him a small plot of our land. You will live with us, but the land will be his. He needs a wife. He spoke of you favorably. Also we have spoken to your mother, and she favors our son and agrees to your marriage."

*What a contrivance,* I said to myself. How could Ilija have spoken of me? We had not seen each other in years, and all that lying about his having a trade—I'll bet. Ilija was not the type to learn anything, I was certain. Further, insofar as my mother's approval, she would pass me off to anyone. How did she dare to voice an opinion of any kind? She didn't know me. Nor did she bother to come along with my grandmother and Sara when they came to see me. I despised her.

To say I was stunned would not accurately describe how I felt. I was numbed. So my time had come, marriage forced upon me. My mind was spinning backward, vividly recalling my earliest observations of Ilija. When he would come to our village to see my brothers and the other boys living around us. Those boys would engage in activities never understood by me. Off to the woods they scampered, yelling, screaming obscenities, beating each other up—becoming men, they called it. They learned well, as generation after generation of males became rough, cruel husbands and fathers. As I said, I never did understand it—still don't, but perhaps it was necessary. Ilija's mouth spewed unspeakable curses. He hated girls; he hated everything. Often I had to dodge a stone aimed at me. Ilija was a handsome boy, I noticed that. He fascinated and repulsed me.

Oh yes indeed, I recalled Ilija's ways, as well as those of my brothers. I suppose the old saying, "Boys will be boys," somehow gives boys permission to do certain unacceptable things and to be generally overlooked. Me, I frankly don't know. Boys are definitely different from girls—in their demeanor, I mean. Practically from the moment of their births and throughout their lives, it seems to me, they exhibit daring, recklessness, and jump, so to speak, before they look. Male personality traits, I decided. My opinion, of course, is based on what I observed in the old country, but I suspect it is universal.

I remember an incident so shocking I am still filled with disgust. Two of my brothers and Ilija, of course, decided to see just what would happen if they tied together the tails of two cows. Having somehow secured the tails together, they switched the cows on their behinds. What happened next was awful. The cows took off in opposite directions, skinning most of the flesh off their tails, leaving one with just a stub of a tail. The cows' bellowing summoned many people to the scene. The sight of the suffering cows quickly led to arguments as to what to do. An old woman, Crista, our village witch, had the solution. Quickly, she organized some people to fetch the necessary ingredients to make poultices for the damaged tails. Someone poured brandy on the tails, but not before the cows were hobbled with ropes. The scene was awful—children crying, adults stunned by such a senseless, cruel act. The worst of it being that the cows did not belong to us. So there was some kind of agreement with my family and the owners that compensation would be made. Perhaps corn, wheat, and eggs—I don't know. Henceforth the boys were reminded of their actions and regularly rebuked.

Well, having mentioned the village witch, I will expand on that. Crista was feared by everyone. It was believed she could cast spells to dry up a cow's milk, cause chickens to stop laying, cause bad luck with the harvest, and bring physical pain and suffering and much more. The list of spells was endless. Villagers accorded her great respect. They often gifted her with food, like chickens and eggs and sometimes wine or brandy, chopped her firewood, or worked in her garden.

Long about my eighth year, I questioned Aunt Danila about the witch. I heard the same story and the same fears. "Why is she not rich?" I asked. "Why does she live in such a hovel? Why does she have no more than any of you? If she had any of the powers she claims she has, should she not be able to conjure up a better house, more chickens, a cow or calf, or anything else she wants? She has managed to put fear in all of you. She is smarter than all of you—and you pay her out of fear. God does not like that."

Danila nearly tripped over a stool as she tried to grab me to put her hand over my mouth. "Child!" she screamed. "If she were to hear you, great misfortune would befall you and the rest of us."

I just stomped outside, muttering, knowing that my aunt would never dare tell anyone of my denouncement of the witch.

Back to the marriage proposal; my future father-in-law spoke, saying he would make all the arrangements for the wedding, and it would take place in his home.

"You must choose a time in the very near future, as we have another wedding to plan. Our daughter, Sofia, is getting married."

"Hah," I said to myself. "A quick plan to marry me off, a quick visit, a quick departure that fits right in with how we do things around here."

My hope was that my favorite peddler, Miroslav, would visit before my wedding. He had wares for women. Twice to three times a year an enterprising peddler or two would take on the back trails to our village. We couldn't classify these trails as roads. They were merely meandering rivers of mud holes, ruts, and rocky stretches, sometimes completely overgrown with grass, yet they overcame all the obstacles, presenting them-selves to a royal welcome and eager buyers. My hope was that Miroslav would come by with his colorful babushkas, fancy combs to decorate one's hair, embroidery thread, and needles for knitting and sewing. On occasion he would show off some silk fabric, actually made in the not-too-far-away cities of our country.

Uncle took any wages I earned as a field hand or weaver when I worked for other families. Therefore I had no money of my own. What I wanted and what I could actually get depended on the devil uncle's frame of mind.

The approaching marriage date was closing in on me, so I needed to augment my woefully inadequate "hope chest," as it is called here in America.

I looked forward to the different wares that the peddler Goran had. He sold tools, shovels, hoes, scythes, nails, grease for wagon wheels, pots and pans, and so on. My fascination with such items lasted all my life. They are essential in a peasant's life. His most notable contribution, however, was that of a letter carrier. He was well read, speaking four languages. Often he would write letters for the villagers or read the ones he brought from the post office from a distant village.

"What is wrong with you people? Still no school. Your children will be just as ignorant as you are. I don't mind writing letters for you or reading the letters I bring, but has it ever occurred to you people to build a schoolhouse and hire a teacher? A schoolmaster could be found in Ogulin. He would gladly accept more work. Once a week would be better than nothing. I talked to you about this before, and I could find someone, but no, I give up. Where is your pride and your concern for your children's future? That should be your first consideration," he mumbled as he departed.

Quite frankly, his words shaming us did not phase me at all. Why should I care? What great good would it bring me? Besides, Goran, I was certain, would continue to take care of such matters. I had no need to write anyone, and who would write to me? I must confess that I was much more fascinated by his wares. Miroslav, in comparison to Goran, seemed so frivolous.

Practically days prior to my marriage, Miroslav showed up with a stock of items that were more beautiful than ever. My devil uncle elevated himself in my judgment of him when he gifted me with a few of the items. Then additionally he gave me a small sum of money, which to me was quite generous. In mid-March, we were wed. The day came and went—there is no part of it that I want to remember, except that I had my first and only pair of harem-style sandals, a gift from my uncle.

# Chapter 11

All that differed in my life now was a male I hoped I could grow to tolerate someday. We were packed into the house like sardines in a can. Two brothers and their two wives, Ilija and I, and the in-laws. The loft overhead was shared by the two brothers and their wives and the stores of grain, flour, dried fruit and vegetables, nuts, and such. Ilija and I had a small space in a corner of the house. Windowless, claustrophobic, and moldy smelling, it could hardly be called the bridal chamber. On the plus side, there was more to eat at the in-laws. They had two cows, an ox, two horses, a large number of chickens, and a pig or two. Other than that, it was still the same austere existence.

The end of the day brought me my greatest dread. Ilija was like some kind of clock—never deviating from his abrupt leap into bed and equally hasty departure for parts unknown. It was better that way—we didn't have to talk. Life was continually dreary as fall settled in. So many sunless days depressed me and still do. My one great relief was when Ilija would abandon our bed for weeks at a time.

Ilija surprised us all when he appeared as we were preparing an evening meal. His father slapped him on the back in greeting and loudly said, "My missing son is here, this is good."

"Not for long," replied Ilija, "I am leaving for America next month."

"Leaving for America? Abandoning us? It's bad enough you leave us shorthanded time after time; now you are going away. Ilija, you are a stupid son. What of Mara?" roared my father-in-law.

"No, no, Mara stays here," said Ilija. "I have no place for her there; I don't even know where I will be. I will send you money when I can spare it. I will return when I have saved up enough money to build my own house."

"How did you hear about work in America?" asked his father.

"Oh, you must have heard about men from America coming to our villages to get workers for the new world. Some time ago, I met such men in Plaski. They need workers, many of them, so I agreed to go to America," explained Ilija.

Well, now Ilija would become one of them. He was proud that he had been recruited. When Ilija left, I was in my fourth month of pregnancy. I had not made an advance announcement to anyone. The bulge in my abdomen in due time would be announcement enough that I was with child.

October is the month of harvest for potatoes in our region. It was evident that the harvest needed to be completed without too much delay, as very cold weather was just ahead. The holes that needed to be dug to store the potatoes in were still waiting to be dug. Ilija's brothers fumed at having to do all the digging without him. In addition, straw was needed to line the holes and to cover the potatoes. It had to be brought to the barn. Hot tempers flared—with swearing to match. My father-in-law quickly settled the matter, saying, "The weather waits for no one, so hurry up, do your work, and shut up."

I was also digging the potatoes, piling them up into small mounds, when suddenly a sharp pain in my lower back made me stagger. My belly heaved up and down. I placed my clasped hands under it for support as I prepared to select a spot for the birthing. That day I happened to be alone in the field. I was happy for that. Quickly I jerked off my apron and snatched the babushka off my head. There was just enough time to spread out the apron on the ground as I dropped to my knees. Pain was increasing, but not unbearable. I was now squatting, knowing that the final moments were at hand. With surprising ease, he arrived—my son. Quickly using the babushka, I cleaned him up. My teeth bit through the cord that would now completely free him from me. He whimpered a time or two as I wrapped him up in my apron and walked home.

My mother-in-law looked up as she knelt next to the fireplace. A new log had just been tossed into the roaring fire.

We needed the warmth. "Bring it here," she said. "What is it? A boy or a girl?"

She held out her arms as I said, "A son. I had a son." Sitting down for a brief while, I tied another apron around my now somewhat smaller waist and returned wordlessly to the potato fields, continuing my day's work.

People in this country may never have heard of such a thing. There it was the system; no one questioned it or challenged it. No prenatal care nor aftercare—you just got pregnant, gave birth, and that was it. We could've used care.

My son was frail from the start. I didn't have enough milk. My mother-in-law soaked bits of cloth soaked in goat milk for him to suck on. Cooked cornmeal, made runny with milk, was spooned into his mouth.

There was little time for me to care for my child. When I did have time for him, he was with me as I worked the loom. He was also with me in the fields, but not too often, as the weight of him slowed me down. That was the best I could do.

Babies were carried about in contrivances made of small tree branches laced up with fabric strips. When I tired, I would remove my baby from my back and suspend his carrier on a tree branch. Flies swirled around his face. What could I do?

The baby struggled through a sickly six months, at which time he mercifully died in June. June still being a cold month and little thawing in the earth, I, myself, dug his grave on a sunny slope behind the house. His was not the only grave there.

Something that haunts me to this day is the circumstance of my son's death. Death was predictable from the beginning, with my not having milk enough to sustain him; the long hours of neglect as I worked in the fields; and leaving him at home with my mother-in-law.

She boasted how well she cared for him, saying, "He never cries when he is with me."

*Of course not, how could he?* I would ask myself. He was probably drugged into oblivion. My people had learned of the effects of opium centuries before. Opium-soaked bits of cloth stuck into the mouths of babes and small children certainly guaranteed a docile child—no troublemaker there.

Opium was used for all manner of ills—imagined or real. When I was questioned by Milka for about the hundredth time, I can comfortably say her reaction was shock as she pressed for more details about her brother as she grew older. "You kept telling me when I was a very little girl that it was poppy milk that was given to him. Now I know what it was."

She was loudly accusing me of being a participant in her brother's death. No amount of explaining that I had no evil intent, but that I was simply going along with the system, could convince her. The subject was never brought up again, thank God.

# Chapter 12

"Bad news travels fast" is probably a well-known saying in most parts of the world. However, in my corner of the world it came slowly. Our first inkling that the Austro-Hungarian Empire had declared war on Serbia in reprisal for the assassination of Archduke Franz Ferdinand, Erzherzog von Österreich-Este, on June 28, 1914, was delivered by a neighboring villager arriving on his donkey's back. His primary purpose for coming was to inform the male Serbs in our village of their duty to their country.

As the Serb peasant minority living in Croatia (in a region called Lika), many of the men felt less than sympathetic to the Serbian cause, simply saying, "We will get to the task in due time." Well, due time was hastened by the appearance of a small detachment of Serbian soldiers who made quick work of rounding up the new recruits. Ilija's brothers were in that group—Ilija had escaped the war.

The slain Archduke, heir to the Austro-Hungarian throne, was shot by a Serbian college student, Gavrilo Princip, one of scores of young Serbian students organized to protest the continued power of the Hapsburgs. Serbia had shed five hundred years of domination by the Turkish Ottoman Empire. The Hapsburgs' power was a difficult pill to swallow after shedding the yoke of the Ottoman Empire. Serbia was struggling to establish herself as a free nation. Even prior to the time of the unfortunate assassination, it was believed that the Hapsburgs needed some kind of incident to provoke a war against Serbia, hoping to develop an even stronger hold on her. Gavrilo Princip provided the Hapsburgs with a perfect, indisputable, set-in-stone event leading to World War I.

There will always be divided opinions of exactly what factors propelled so many nations into one more devastating war.

The war was not exactly on our doorstep; however, we believed it would only be a matter of time. Being out of touch with the outside world, we had no clue from which direction we would be overrun. From past experience, those who were old enough to remember said it would be without a doubt the deserting armies who would be the scourge of defenseless people. Food and shelter would be their first priorities, followed by the classic behavior of such invaders who pillage, murder, and rape.

The war was in its second year, 1915. Just one or two soldiers skulking along the dense forest's edge was warning enough that more would follow.

The old men of the village were ready for them. Lookouts had been designated. A preplanned system of alert had also been put in place. Shots would ring out; sometimes a cow's bell would send up a clatter. What did it mean? Most of us had no idea. The elders merely let it be known that the fewer of us knowing the details, the more successful their plan to protect the village would be. Little comfort came from any such assurances. Every now and then there would be a lull, then a few soldiers would appear, then another period of time passed, and we saw none. The old men of the village, we later learned, patrolled at night, capturing and killing the wandering soldiers. Terror reigned supreme at sightings of the soldiers.

One particular day there had been a commotion at the far edge of the village. Soka and Marina, my sisters-in-law, and I were too frightened to venture far from the house to see what it was all about. The cow bells had sounded, continuing their clanking for quite a while. Was it a signal to hide or dash or what?

A quick decision was made to drop whatever we were doing and hasten up into our hiding place in the loft. What we had thought of as being another overnight stay up there in the loft, or perhaps a day or so at the most, turned into a most confusing and perplexing time. Recalling exactly the details of those days is impossible. After several days without food or water, we easily slipped into a state of weakness. I do remember Soka, the youngest, babbling incoherently, stumbling about, and finally, falling into a deep sleep. We could not awaken her. It was clear that the same fate would overtake us as well.

"It's the hunger; we will die," I hoarsely whispered.

Fear that the enemy was still among us didn't seem to matter much. We had mostly been sitting or lying down, fearful that the slightest sound would reveal our hiding place. Marina could only weakly lift her hand, indicating that she had heard me.

Marina later said I had become boisterous before falling down through the open hatch. The fall didn't even faze me, I was told. The girls had managed to haul me back up. The waking-up process took a while; I don't know how long. The passage of time could not be measured.

Finally, weak and dazed, we emerged, having decided that death in the outside world would be preferable. It seems no one had noticed our absence. However, something quite remarkable was happening. Villagers had banded together for the purpose of survival. Some of them had decided to hunt in the forest. Game was plentiful. Caution was thrown to the wind. Several spits had been erected over the coal beds, which were heavy with deer; a most festive atmosphere prevailed as neighbors embraced each other, singing and dancing. A couple of soldiers joined us. For one reason or another, they had escaped the wrath of the village men, perhaps because they were so very young. All this time my in-laws' absence told us that they had decided to leave the village and were in hiding somewhere.

My sisters in-law and I were the only ones left at the homestead. Their husbands were rounded up and led away with the other young men to become part of the army. Immediately after learning of the attack on Serbia, the village women quietly, almost invisibly, contacted each other to formulate some plan of defense of our own. Death was more desirable then rape, we all agreed. We feigned illness or kept ourselves soiled with feces or urine in the desperate hope that it would deter some crazed soldier. Rape, the ultimate loss of oneself, dictated strong measures.

Hiding food stores was difficult—spoilage could claim it all. Most families were secretive as to how or where they hid their food. Fear and distrust of a neighbor was equal to the fear of the invaders, should they come.

When we realized the in-laws had left, it was our first instinct to see what they might have taken with them. Of course, what else? Most of the food was gone. Now we had to hide what was left. Soka, Marina, and I dug into the hard-packed dirt inside the barn, under the hay. We worked under cover of night, wearing dark clothes as sack by sack we buried the grain. Wheat, millet, corn, rye—we had so little of it to begin with—and we realized that the in-laws had reduced the stores, taking them when they left.

Three or four days later, after hiding our grain, we almost simultaneously declared, "Oh, we've made a grave mistake."

Soka was becoming unraveled as she started to sob and wail. "We're going to feed every rat, squirrel, and who knows what else."

"You are right," I said. "How could we be so stupid? What do we do now? Let's not moan; Old Branko is the one who can tell us what to do. We can trust him. He is wise, and besides, so many of our men go to him for advice. Hurry up, let's go quickly, right now."

Old Branko was indeed some kind of man—set apart from the others. He lived alone for as long as I could recall—never in my life had I been close enough to see his face. All I knew about him was what I could, on rare occasions, observe from a distance. A tall, white-bearded man, slightly stooped yet powerful looking, he walked with confidence. Village men tilled his small plot of ground, planting and harvesting it as well. He had a few fruit trees and a grape arbor. Often as he sat under a tree he would be reading and sometimes writing, the only literate person in the village. His reputation as the wise one was known to all, even the children. Branko read to them quite often as they sat at his feet. Boy, did we need some of that wisdom right then. A timid knock on his door, and there he was. Now I could see deeply set eyes of the bluest blue I had ever seen.

"Oh," he said jovially. "Young ladies at my door. Such a lovely sight. What can I do for you? Come in. Sit down; tell me what I can do." Our story was listened to as an occasional hum passed his lips. "Yes, ladies, a change has to be made immediately. I'll tell you what to do."

The change was another backbreaking undertaking. A small cave at the corner of our land was known to Branko. How he knew of it we never thought to ask. We wedged small sacks in the uneven cave's ceiling, then sprinkled poppy seed powder below. How that could help, we did not ask. As good fortune would have it, my sisters-in-law had considerable fabric that they had made and wanted to hide. I too had a nice collection of fabric that I had hidden from my father-in-law, knowing that he would otherwise claim it and sell it. Our plan developed quickly as we devised a way to hide our collective fabrics, believing that at wars-end, we could sell off the fabric which would surely be in short supply in the village by then.

Hiding fabric in the barn was not a good idea. So again, at night we took turns carrying a few bundles at a time to the cave. Without so much as a candle or a lantern, we carried out our work. Each nook and cranny of the cave had been memorized. In the blackness, we fought fear of what creature could attack us. Youth was a great help, as we often laughed at the dangers of our mission. Stones and branches obscured the cave's opening. Once in a while we would walk to that area, satisfying ourselves that it was still undisturbed.

We three nightly hid in the overhead loft, pulling the ladder up out of sight. We put up a supply of food that we could eat just in case it was dangerous to come out of hiding. Finally the dreaded soldiers began to appear in the spring of 1916. Soldiers from different European nations were systematically abandoning the front battle lines and showing up in our village. Mostly they skirted the village, seeking refuge in the woods during the day. At night they would venture out, sizing up the area, no doubt. Some must have sensed the potential danger of being too visible. No shots were fired by them. Often times the villagers offered food, hoping to forestall some aggressive action by the soldiers.

Trying to live as normal a life as possible was necessary, as the fields needed attention. We planted and harvested, all the while praying for it all to end. As slowly as we had learned of the beginning of the conflict, we slowly learned about its end.

We had kept the fabric's existence a secret. As time went on, we knew we would do well to sell off some of it. We were more than a little surprised when some peddlers showed up, wanting to buy the fabric. Word of mouth cannot be underestimated, as the constant question to ourselves was, "How did they know?" How they heard about us was not important. However, we did not trust these men. So reluctantly, we consulted our father-in-law as to the best way to protect ourselves and the fabric.

He had returned with his wife, and we seemingly returned to normal, he never explaining nor we ever asking where they had gone. He was pleased and impressed with us. He seemed to be filled with admiration. He was a formidable force, just what was needed. Bargaining was his strength—we felt he had done a good job for us all. My suggestion that he be compensated for his role really pleased him. There were no objections from the others. We did not sell off all of our fabrics and didn't really know how to protect it. Distrust was rampant, probably due to the fear of some kind of reprisal from the villagers.

The political forces in power were beyond our village, yet we feared being watched. Our situation was precarious; we were always reminding ourselves we were Serbs, a minority in Croatian territory. For the most part, the two groups of people were sharing a language prior to the war, separated by religious differences but living in harmony. We knew our place. Making trouble for ourselves was carefully avoided. After the war both sides sought a peaceful coexistence, harkening back to the old days.

# Chapter 13

As time went on, I developed many skills to the point of perfection. That statement makes me smile; humility never got anyone recognition. The production of fabric gave me the status of "the one with golden hands." Let me tell you all about it. Our village was so remotely situated in a very mountainous region that very little trade with the outside world took place. Being impoverished further separated us from the world beyond. Don't waste any pity on our circumstances. Deprivation can teach valuable lessons of survival.

So it was that to produce the needed fabrics, one needed to be skilled and speedy as well. Only two fibers were available to us: wool for warmth and linen for all the other general fabric needs.

Wool was simpler to produce. Sheering sheep, carding, spinning into thread, and finally weaving into a durable fabric was the process. Most of the woolen fabric was left natural, undyed. Some was dyed black, necessitating no maintenance whatsoever, worn till it fell into shreds. Red was a welcomed color, mostly for embellishment and an occasional fashion statement. But who could afford fashion? Where did I hear that expression?

Now I can tell you about the second fiber. Linen, linen, linen, linen, which to my last days on this planet is still remembered with a shudder and represented a challenge that I could not walk away from. Plowing the field that was to receive the flax seed was step number one.

Incidentally, women of all ages, from youngest to the eldest, pushed the plow through rock-strewn ground. Yes, the female, the drudge, the lowest-classed person in the structure of the village society toiled in the fields. Men could be seen at the kafana where they would be playing cards, telling the same old tales of wartime and conquests of the stupid female. A great deal of drinking and swearing took place. To me it seemed that their most notable contribution was increasing the population. Nevertheless, I to this day take pride in my survival and my tenacious resolve to do my job and to do it well—very well indeed.

Step number two: after tending the plants, carrying water from the creek when rain was scarce and then harvesting

Step number three: carrying the flax crop to the creek, which was prepared in advance to create small dams surrounded by rocks. The cut stalks of flax were securely held down by still more rocks, remaining submerged until the outer layer became soft enough to strip away. This exposed the usable strands, now ready to be made into a thread, which at that point had to be dried before they were possible to work with.

Step number four was making the thread. Picture this as I tell you about the most tortuous part of the process. Pain I still vividly can recall on demand as I put a hand to my lips to assure myself that linen making is part of the long-ago past. We did not have the advanced knowledge of how flax was transformed into a thread. Our method was what I call Stone Age primitive. Women of the village took turns at each other's homes to assist in this process.

The long fibers were first twisted between the thumbs, the index fingers, and the middle fingers to give them shape and length. The twisted length of fibers was passed through one's lips, all the while using saliva to "glue" the fibers together. A second person carefully rolled up the fiber into one long, continuous thread.

At the end of three to four days, the agony of split and splinter-filled lips was so excruciatingly painful that a sip of water was enough to make a person weak-kneed. The end was not yet in sight; weaving followed.

Our looms were functional, yet primitive, as I learned later. It was backbreaking work, lasting weeks till all the thread was utilized. I had a talent—I must brag on myself. The rows of thread were closely compacted and perfectly straight. In later years in this country, I was labeled a compulsively exacting person, or something like that. All I know is that I just had to do it right. It was near impossible to produce linen threads that were uniform in size or texture. Yet I could produce an enviable product. The finished woven product was so stiff that a narrow width of fabric two feet in length could practically stand up by itself. A softer fabric would be returned to the creek, beaten with green, flexible tree branches, and made suitable for use on an infant's tender body. Some diapers, huh? Softer fabrics were used for shirts, blouses, babushkas, and so on.

Yet life was tolerable. I was not alone. It was the system.

# Chapter 14

$\mathcal{I}$n all the passing years since Ilija's departure, I never heard anything of him. Of course, I was illiterate, as was he, yet letters crossed the ocean if one took the time and trouble to find someone literate to write a letter for you. Often I questioned my in-laws about my husband. Of course, they said they knew nothing, but I did not believe that.

At one point I had asked one of the elders in a neighboring village, a man named Milan, who had attended school—as to where people of power were to be found. He said, "Go to Plaski" which was a three-day walk from our village. The information he provided me with remained filed away in my brain, eventually giving birth to a travel plan.

Both of my sisters-in-law came from families of plenty with more land, livestock, and such. As one would expect, their families provided clothing, footwear, and blouses, all kinds of stuff I longed for. They were pretty good at flaunting such gifts in the faces of our in-laws.

So when I confided in them that I would be appearing before some official in an attempt to locate Ilija, they kept my secret and gifted me with a few articles of clothing, and best of all, shoes. It never crossed my mind that I would need to make a better appearance by wearing shoes. I only put on the shoes just before entering the building. I did not want to damage them on my three-day trek on foot. Spending nights in accommodating strangers' barns, I finally found myself standing in front of an imposing building matching Milan's description. I was in Plaski, which was equivalent to a county seat in America. My idea of an imposing building at that time in my life was a structure larger than a barn. Ours were not that big.

Upon entering, I looked about to find someone to speak to. A man approached me, sensing that I was a misplaced person.

"Where can I find someone who could help me find my husband in America?" I blurted out.

He ushered me into an office. Sitting across the desk from a very distinguished man dressed in garb that I had never seen before, I was at once impressed but felt unsure of myself. However, I summoned up my courage and stated my case clearly and firmly. My husband, Ilija, had abandoned me ten and a half years ago when he left for America. We never heard from him again. I had become my in-laws' indentured servant. My father-in-law took all my earnings as a field hand and weaver for others. My greatest sorrow was the death of my son after Ilija left. Ilija knew I was with child when he left. Mister Mondich patiently asked questions relating to my in-laws, their names, where they lived, my maiden name, and much, much more. As I listened to and answered questions, I felt doomed.

What could my answers achieve?

"So, young woman, you have given almost eleven years of your life to those selfish, cruel people. They stole your freedom and deprived you of your wages as a field hand and a weaver, and you have suffered great indignities at their hands. I will change all of that and we will find Ilija, dead or alive. First, you return home and give to your father-in-law a document I will prepare. The document will demand that he appear before me within two weeks. Should he be unwilling to do so, I will dispatch the police to fetch him. You will be released from this bondage even if it should be found that your husband is dead," said Mister Mondich.

My feet barely touched the ground. My heart singing, spirits soaring, I envisioned all sorts of exciting scenarios about a wonderful, happy life in America. *Ilija, here I come.*

The loud reaction to the document and what I had dared to do could be termed as cataclysmic in nature. Milan had read it to my father-in-law.

"You are an ungrateful whore. You have been unfaithful to my son; why would he want you? It is questionable that he was the father of your son. I will defend my actions vigorously. I will be believed. I punished you as I saw its need. You are nothing, do you hear?" screamed my father-in-law. My ears hardly took in the tirade; I was that certain that the words spoken by Mr. Mondich were a guarantee of my freedom.

To say that there was an exodus of people, all following my father-in-law in carts and on horse and muleback as we left for Plaski, is to truly minimize the scene. Mostly men, very few women, journeyed to the courthouse. There was laughter as well as ridicule. Who does Mara think she is? She is an upstart seeking to disrupt the accepted way of doing things.

To briefly summarize the historic event, my father-in-law was forced to divulge the whereabouts of his son, Ilija, and to admit that there had been letters crossing the ocean often enough to provide accurate information as to where Ilija lived and worked. "In the meantime, you will grant this young woman the same rights as you would your sons. She is free to live in your home, to seek work, to keep her wages, and furthermore, you are to accord her the respect she deserves. If I hear anything to the contrary, you will be jailed here under my jurisdiction," intoned Mr. Mondich.

In a few weeks, a letter had been sent to Milan instructing him to contact me, as I was to return to the courthouse. Mr. Mondich was making my journey back a much more pleasant one. He was sending a horse-drawn conveyance for me. Further, I was to bring along extra clothing, as it would take a day or two to prepare additional documents.

Once I was home again, things were cool but peaceful. I could live with that. As I awaited word of my husband's whereabouts, I learned of a devastating setback. That I never realized that it would take a great deal of money to travel to America made me feel like a stupid fool. The letter suggested that I personally appeal to my father-in-law for some portion of my wages that he had appropriated, or I was to work, save money, and notify by letter when I had the necessary money in hand. Mr. Mondich had provided information as to the sum of money that I might need, saying that additional expenses that he could not predict could arise.

My father-in-law astounded me when he agreed upon a settlement, giving me a goodly portion of the needed cash. I knew that his motivation was to get rid of me. Six months later, I had the whole amount. As I recall I judged it to be a fortune considering the year: 1922.

My application for permission to travel was granted August 28, 1923. It was mailed to Plaski. Milan had traveled to alert the post office that important papers would be sent to me care of that post office. He asked the postmaster to safeguard the papers and to appoint some individual as a courier for the express purpose of a safe delivery to me. Now I was ready. So when the permission to travel documents were read by Milan, my mind geared up for the trip.

All of those paper transactions took time and a lot of back and forth. Finally, with my passport and visa in hand, I began to sleep poorly, dreaming of very strange events. I began to think the dreams were harbingers of bad things to come.

Milan made arrangements for wagon transportation to Plaski, where I would board a train to Zagreb, capital of Croatia. A small wooden trunk and a canvas duffel bag held all that I owned. Milan obtained these items for me in Plaski before I was due to

leave. I was able to reimburse him. I could never repay his kindness and attention to all the details of the paperwork. He was
genuinely pleased that I would be one of the fortunate ones that
left for the new world.

There was still one final requirement: a physical examination.
What that would entail was a mystery to me. I had never in my
life seen a doctor. The time and place were prearranged by Milan,
so all I had to do was to present myself when I arrived in Plaski.
A tiny house squeezed in between a barbershop and a meatery,
as the butcher shop was called, painted an ugly green, was the
doctor's office. That was it. Once inside, strange smells assailed
my nose. Later, I learned that ether was the offender. There were
others also waiting, looking glum. Sick patients, I guessed. Finally
I was summoned by a large, buxom woman wearing some sort of
odd-looking covering on her head. She asked my name and if I
had any papers for the doctor. I produced the permission to travel
document, and she disappeared. Soon I was in the presence of an
ordinary-looking, middle-aged man with a huge beard and untidy
whiskers. He looked kind, smiling as he read my document.

"Oh, Marija," (my full name in Serbian) "I see you will be
leaving us. You can return, you do know that, don't you? This
paper says so. By the way, I am Doctor Bukovich. This will be
an easy examination, but I do need to ask you some questions."

With a nod to his assistant, I was led away to a small cubicle
and instructed to remove my clothes and don a white garment.
Now before the doctor, I prepared myself for whatever—I didn't

know what. He studied my eyes for a while, pressing the lids against the eyeballs, pulling the lids up, and asking if I had any discomfort. "Your teeth," he said, "are healthy. No rotten teeth—very good. Your throat looks good; now let me listen to your heart." An odd-looking apparatus was used for this part of the examination. "Lungs and heart are good too," he declared. There were other procedures, noninvasive, as they often are today.

Then the examination turned into something of an intense interrogation. First of all, was I leaving of my own free will? Did I swear that I was not an indentured servant? Was I free of debt? Was I a woman of high morals? Was I a professional prostitute? Was I a polygamist? Was I a member, now or in the past, of a group that was unfriendly to or critical of the government or that taught rebellion against the government? Finally, was I ever arrested? Believe me, the questions were unnerving. Suddenly I realized that I was a good person, a decent citizen of the country of my birth. I vowed to myself I would be equally proud of myself in my new country. The doctor applied his signature. The date was September 27, 1923.

He escorted me to the door and pointed out the train station, saying, "Of course, you cannot miss it. I just want to make sure that you see it from here. Right now you seem a bit overwhelmed and nervous. I am confident you will find your way to your final destination."

The train station was small, but well staffed, I noticed. Clerks were talking to people about their destinations, selling tickets, and stamping whatever it was that required stamping. Soon it was my turn at the ticket window. I couldn't find my voice at first. The clerks spoke crisply yet politely, asking to see my papers. I quickly snapped to attention and took care of business, you could say.

Being illiterate, I certainly couldn't read any of that stuff, but I had memorized everything with Milan's tutoring. He had repeatedly emphasized the importance of committing to memory the information in those papers. I wondered how I could do that. Yet, as I tested my memory day by day, I grew confident. My future depended on my memory. So I had to do it. Not being able to read, I had actually committed all that stuff to memory, astonishing Milan every time he came to out village to check on me.

My first train ride. Imagine the amazement I felt. This ponderous thing spewing steam and belching black smoke began to jerk forward, faltering a bit, picking up a little speed, then jerking some more, and we were finally clear of the train yard. At first I couldn't tell if we were moving, or the countryside was whizzing past. The rocking of the car and the sound of the wheels on the track kept me focused. I was afraid I would miss something. My passport was examined and stamped as we crossed borders to other countries. The scenery was spectacular, with glimpses of people on farms—all looking better than ours, truly a lovely sight.

Hours passed; finally the train stopped. A wave of a conductor's hand directed passengers to a place where we could have a meal and overnight lodgings. I could not have prepared myself for that experience. There was nothing in my past to compare it to.

Large, long tables, laden with food, awaited us. I wondered how I would pay for this. Oh, my God, plates, forks, spoons, knives. Everyone I saw was obviously acquainted with how to use these things. I was awkward at first, but after a while, I became a pro. At meal's end, what struck me was that, with each new experience, I was that much further from my village, and that comforted me.

Passengers asked questions in their assorted tongues sometimes successful in explaining their questions but most times not. Nevertheless, it all fell into place somehow.

We were ushered upstairs, paired off with others of our own sex, and assigned a room. That, too, worked out without too much difficulty. I slept with my traveling clothes on, kicking off my shoes and tying a babushka around my hair so as not to mess it up. Imagine a bed long enough to accommodate my stretched-out body. It was somewhat lumpy, but the mattress was far superior to a straw pallet. The down cover and pillow were stale smelling. The softness, though, dispelled any aversion I had to sleeping on other people's beds.

There were more such stops. All were pretty much the same. That made it easier for me to cope. Although I must say, I was beginning to enjoy the adventure. There was such a sense of freedom, of not having any strings attached. I did worry about my dwindling cash. Someone told me that we had left Austria, been to Germany, and would sail from France. Each night the food and lodgings were quite similar. Each establishment teemed with travelers. There were men, women, and children—all weary looking and harried—yet an excitement filled the air.

I learned that all of us were America bound. I was looking forward to sailing, mostly because that would be the last part of my journey. There was some apprehension, as I had heard of ships sinking, drowning people, and all of that. I realized there was no way around it. What we didn't know then was about fast luxury ships and airplanes. We would not have believed if we had been told about such things.

Along the way, listening to conversations here and there, I would pick up on familiar words and phrases. Many of them were being stored away in my brain—a real help in taking care of myself. Yugoslav, or Serbo-Croatian, as my language is most commonly referred to, was not too often heard, but Austrian and German were becoming quite familiar to my ear. Therefore, my level of comfort increased daily.

Before long I could interact with others. Garbled sentences, lots of hand gestures, lots of laughter—lots of happiness for me. Sometimes I would actually lose sight of the fact that my journey, now so enjoyable, would end. All these people I'd grown to like were just passing through my life.

Many would be remembered forever. Like the woman with three young children I had met on the train from Plaski to Zagreb. Of course, just the experience of boarding that first train going where, I had no idea, was enough to clam me up. A stranger was always someone to be watchful of, even a woman with children.

Actually, looking back now, I realize that she could not do me harm. Surely I must've known that. It was just the contrast in us that made me uncomfortable.

There she was, a young woman surrounded by three bright, outgoing children, gaily chatting with them, playfully teasing them—such astonishing behavior, I thought. Their language was unfamiliar to me. It was just as well. I didn't want her to know anything about me anyway. All I needed to know about her I could see. I would look away, as they seemed so unreal; I felt a hunger, a feeling of loneliness and abandonment. My eyes were closed as my breath and heartbeat returned to normalcy, as I had feared my emotions would expose me. I wished I could just sleep away the sight that alternately pleased and pained me. Would I ever be a mother such as her?

Then, lost in my thoughts, eyes still closed, I felt a soft touch on my arm and heard a small voice say, "Madam." Startled, I saw the eldest of the children, a girl about ten or twelve years old. Quickly she backed away, returning to her mother's seat.

"Ah, madam," said the mother as she held out an apple in her hand. What else she said was lost on me. But the apple, followed by a delicious piece of cheese, made her my friend forever.

On the fifth day of my train journey, the word "France" in many variations of pronouncement was called out. "Ah, France," I said to myself. "My boat awaits somewhere on your shores.

On October 6, 1923, I boarded the SS *Barrengaria* in Charbourg, France, owned by the Cunard Steamship Company, Ltd. Such a mass of bodies at the train station. Disembarking the train was a bit worrisome, and I became concerned about my luggage. First the tag on my coat was examined by someone looking very official, and then someone waived me in the direction of a long line of waiting people. There was a clamor of mothers and fathers frantically calling out their children's names, clutching them, restraining them, and holding them tight—this was no place to lose a child.

Not all the humanity looked so frantic and displaced. Others, seasoned travelers I assumed, quietly, purposefully moved here and there with confidence. It was a short distance to the seaport in Charbourg from the small inn where I had spent one and a half days

Every phase of getting travelers from place to place was well orchestrated. I don't think anyone was misplaced or left behind.

The people who took care of all the details of passports, visas, and other documents were businesslike and efficient. They were obviously well trained to handle all manner of people—for some of us were clearly crazy. Not all travelers could bear the stress of leaving for America. It was not an unusual sight to witness the collapse of a person in their tracks, incoherent and wailing. Thinking about it even now gives me a headache. Paperwork concluded, luggage loaded onto a horse-drawn conveyance, the travelers were taken to the docking area.

The sight of the ship caught me off guard. I kept saying, "Oh my God, oh my God." There was a loud chorus of voices—probably saying the same thing. How could I have imagined something so mammoth in size? People on the decks were waving and calling out. We were ushered into a long waiting line of people, who at a snail's pace were going up the gang plank. In spite of the confusion, we were greeted by official-looking persons who checked our tickets, passports, and visas. In my case, as in others I saw, our tags were checked and our identities verified and such.

Oh, my God, at this point I must tell you of the men who so amazed me. First of all they were very dark skinned with the whitest teeth that simply dazzled me. They wore bright-red jackets with a little bit of white shirt showing, black pants, and very shiny black shoes. Oh, yes, shiny buttons I believed to be gold were fastened on the jacket and the sleeves. I simply gawked, looking like a fool, I guessed; yep, you guessed it: my first introduction to an African-French person. They represented more to me than helpers as I saw their job of expediting the handling of personal belongings. Their persona was impressive as I envied their freedom to laugh, to kindly direct the sea of people to the right places to be. They seemed to be above the craziness and confusion. I wanted to know more about them.

After what seemed like hours, I was ushered into a long compartment with bunks and a place for luggage. By the time we were ready to sail, my niche was occupied by three more women and an infant. Between our assorted native tongues we managed to communicate well enough to be of some assistance to one another.

Seasickness among passengers was bad. I luckily escaped it. Tending to those less fortunate was good for me. People, no matter what their background, do appreciate a helping hand.

We mingled with other passengers from time to time. Fresh air on the decks assigned to us had the same fresh air as the first-class decks, someone laughingly remarked. We were happy enough. The baby added to the optimism we tried to maintain.

Our journey lasted six days. When the seas were turbulent, I feared we would overturn and sink. Even in fair weather, when on deck, I avoided looking at the sea. It made me very uneasy. I have always had a dread of drowning since my childhood.

The last year that shipping lines were allowed to book people in steerage accommodations was in 1922. Thank goodness I sailed in 1923. I missed the horrors of traveling in steerage. I heard all about it some years after my arrival in America. People were packed in like sardines. Small bunks and crowded, smelly compartments accommodated six to eight people. No privacy. They shared chamber pots, and the food was poorly cooked, and there was not much of it. There was no daylight—they were never allowed up on a deck. Illness was common. Death as well. Thank God for the laws that put a stop to such traveling.

The laws and regulations governing immigration into America were unknown to me at that time. Eventually, when I learned of the many statesmen, political figures, and legal battles that raged for and against admission of certain people, I was grateful to be one of the fortunate allowed to enter and to stay in America.

Senator Henry Cabot Lodge, in a speech before Congress in 1897, argued that literacy tests for immigrants should be enforced, declaring that the low class of poor, illiterate people coming into the country, particularly from Eastern Europe, was bringing down the standard of living that many Americans were enjoying. He further argued that the doors to America should be closed to those kinds of people, the discards of their own countries.

President Grover Cleveland vetoed Cabot's bill on March 2, 1897. I was only four years old at that point in time.

More objections to the continued arrival of Eastern Europeans led to the first quota laws in 1921. England was granted the highest quota limits of seventy thousand plus persons annually. Germany's quota was about sixty-five thousand. Then the numbers dwindled to merely two to five thousand for countries like Greece, Portugal, Belgium, Hungary, Yugoslavia, and others from which hundreds of thousands had already immigrated to American shores. The arguments on both sides of immigration issues continued. Should America continue to accept Eastern Europeans or not?

I recommend that everyone read the second edition of *Coming to America* by Roger Daniels to learn about the impact of immigrants, past and present. I cite his figures on quotas.

By 1923, the year I was admitted to America, the quota for my region included this poor, uneducated soul. Not a day passes that I am not grateful that not only was I rescued, but my child was born in this country, and her four children as well. Had I failed in my quest, I might have perished in the increasingly harsh circumstances of my homeland.

Europe's centuries-old conflicts, fired by religious and political factions, destroyed governments, lands, and the economy itself, spawning a population of peasantry, hopelessly uneducated and destitute.

Then along came recruiters from America seeking laborers for the growing expansion of America's industrialization. The poor of Europe were on the top of the list. Promises of jobs and housing were enticing. Their passage was paid by the companies who recruited them, further making the offer more attractive.

These recruits were sent to regions in America, wherever there were labor shortages. In my lifetime, having met countless immigrants, all I ever heard was, "We are grateful for admittance to America. In spite of the hardships we encountered, life was far better in America. Our greatest wealth was the opportunities our children enjoyed. Freedom, education, free choices of religions, and political ties. So much more than we could have ever imagined." Yes, gratitude—it humbles one. When looking back the places from whence we had come, thank you, America.

My husband, Ilija, was recruited by the meat-packing industry, along with several other men from our village. Later I learned he was wooed away by a mining company with promises of more pay and good housing. I think we have all heard a song with the lyrics, "I owe my soul to the company store." This was actually a quote I heard in West Virginia long before the song became popular.

# Chapter 15

*W*ord spread quickly that we were nearing the harbor where we would disembark. Crowds filled the passageways as word that we would be passing a most memorable sight created a stir of excitement. We passengers crowded every inch of the deck like ants. Shouts and pointing directed my eyes to the most amazing sight I'd ever seen.

A huge, unbelievably huge, figure of a woman holding something in her upraised hand brought tears to my eyes. At that time how could I know that she was welcoming us, each and every one, as she had for so many years before? How could I know that the object in her hand was a torch? I'd never seen one before. And that it lit our way to a new life. I felt very moved—the tears flowed. I didn't know any of her history or her purpose, so that was not what made me cry. It was the amazement that a woman was important enough, obviously respected, majestically idealized enough to be displayed so gloriously. Where I came from, that could never happen.

We were transferred to a smaller ship to get closer to the docking area at Ellis Island.

Ellis Island—what an ocean of humans undulating, flowing, sometimes whipped up as though by a strong relentless wind. People pulling, pushing, some crying. The din was awful. If I believed that my head was muddled before with all the train changes, strange meals, and sometimes skimpy accommodations, I was not prepared for that noise. The sound was burrowing straight into my brain. Life in the old country could be deathly quiet lots of times. But this noise, so filled with human emotions, could send a person over the edge.

I need not have worried myself, for help was at hand. Men and women—some of the ladies looked like nurses—circulated among us. Some held up signs in different languages, assuring us that our needs would soon be taken care of. Milan's words came to mind as he had once assured me that travelers would be assisted—and we were.

Reasonable quiet and order were implemented. We were directed to form lines that were sectioned off by railings, like a maze. I didn't know what a maze was then. There was a great deal I did not know. We followed the leader until every person was eventually sent to an enclosed area that turned out to be a clinic. There were nurses and doctors questioning, examining, probing, and poking bodies. It seemed that a great many people were physically and emotionally spent. They were separated from the rest and directed elsewhere.

While awaiting my turn, I noticed the eyes were thoroughly examined, sometimes by more than one medical person. Pink eye, or conjunctivitis, was reason enough to quarantine an individual until it cleared up. Without antibiotics, then unknown, the condition did not always respond to a boric acid wash. Whole families had to wait out the recovery of one of their kin. If the condition did not clear up, those poor unfortunates were returned to their origins.

Tuberculosis was carefully screened for as well.

People in quarantine or any kind of detention were charged for food and lodging in the clinic. Some were cleaned out, left destitute. Greedy, heartless employees swindled people unable to protect themselves. Unread, uneducated people made up the biggest mass of those so dealt with. Seems no place on Earth is safe from such lowlifes.

I heard, but did not know if the rumor was true, that a desperate couple with children had chosen to destroy themselves rather than return to their homeland. The story was that each of the parents, with a child in their arms, had jumped overboard as soon as they were back on the ship, still moored in the harbor. It was a terrible tragedy. I still wonder if it truly happened.

God had spared me. I passed the physical examinations. More paperwork. Again standing in lines, awaiting the final processing of paperwork, I could see the scene of anger and desk pounding. Seems the problem was conveying to those in charge what our names were and how they were spelled. When it was my turn, I found myself clearly pronouncing my name, "Marija Opsenica."

I could not spell it because I spoke no English, and I was illiterate in my own language. All the response that I got was the shaking of a head. I fared better than most. My name was shortened to Opas, Opez, and Opesa. Take your pick.

It did, however, cause many problems during my lifetime. At various times, these strange spellings appeared on documents. Exasperation! Some new papers were added to the ones I already had. What happened to me and countless thousands of others not speaking English was a surprise—a big surprise. Names were changed, completely altered, and misspelled. In general, the whole matter of accurately identifying us was handled in a most cavalier manner.

I will agree that those assigned to the jobs were not too educated, themselves. People numbering in the thousands poured into America. Ships were arriving in the harbor at fifteen-minute intervals, discharging as many as ten thousand immigrants each. A fact I learned decades later. It was a huge undertaking for any agency to deal with. Mistakes were made—a small price to pay for being allowed to stay.

Believe it or not, I was so numbed by the voyage that once inside the Ellis Island compound I took no notice of my surroundings. Not even the great hall, in its splendor, registered with me. Not until I was able to sit down on a bench, waiting for the next phase of processing, did I look up at a sight so breathtaking I thought I was dreaming. There was a great arched ceiling. "So this is America," I said to myself. "I would've come all this way just to see this and the woman in the harbor."

For three days I stayed in a dormitory until train transportation could be arranged for me. There was a small charge for that accommodation. However, I spent one long day again being processed and tagged like a piece of luggage, then transferred by carriage to a train station before boarding a train bound for a place called Fairmont, West Virginia.

# Chapter 16

The train chugged along for two days, making many stops. I experienced hunger—such hunger. Not knowing how to ask for something to eat, as food was brought aboard by vendors, I grew weak and light-headed.

Finally, a blessed woman, a stranger, beckoned me to come to her seat. She tried to communicate with me, but to no avail. She pressed into my hand two pieces of bread with a thin slice of meat and cheese; I was introduced to my first sandwich. Such generosity! I was amazed. I felt that I was dreaming—that this was happening to me again. The woman had children, two of them. Surely they needed the food for themselves. An egg, hard-boiled, followed by a black plum. I was stuffed to the point of discomfort—pleasant discomfort.

Finally, at my destination, I presumed, I was ushered off the train. My tag checked with my luggage close at my side, I was now a passenger on a fine horse-drawn conveyance, the likes of which I had never seen. The seats were far more comfortable than they looked. The seats were padded, covered in a fabric of an interesting design. Such luxury I could not conceive of. What kind of fabric was this? And was it so plentiful that people actually sat upon it in a public place? My fascination with fabric later, but not too much later, became a mania that still draws me to a fabric store.

I was transferred to another carriage, this one by no means luxurious, fancy, or comfortable. I noticed the farmlands with white houses, red barns, and silos—a heretofore never seen structure of unknown function. After a while we were surrounded by steep hills. There were mountains in the not-too-far distance. The farmlands disappeared, now being replaced by dingy, small houses surrounded by equally small plots of ground. There were remnants of what may have been vegetable gardens of the past summer and a few fruit trees; it was definitely a land of plenty, I thought.

What a buggy ride from the train station to Fairmont, West Virginia. Fatigue and sleepiness dimmed some recollections of that trip till a jerky stop, nearly knocking me off my seat, let me know that I might have reached my destination. We had stopped in front of a shabby-looking house at the end of a dusty road.

The driver appeared tired himself as he gingerly stepped down from his seat. Methodically, he lifted my belongings one piece at a time, roughly dumping them next to the steps of the house. As he was turning to board his buggy, I yelled at him. He paused and I rushed up to him, grabbing his sleeve with one hand and my tag with the other. I started a tirade of words, none of which he could understand, gesturing toward the house and pointing to myself.

Did he understand my situation? I kept asking him. To this point there was always someone to direct me to the right places to go. Now this uncomprehending man was merely going to abandon me. He was jerking away from me, gesturing, and answering me in kind. I understood not a single word he was saying. He bounded up the steps and then loudly banged on the door, muttered something, then banged a few more times. There was no response, so he came down to where I was waiting, waved his arm, saying more of nothing I could understand, and boarded his buggy, leaving me standing there. Obviously I could assume that no one was at home. Sitting on one of the lower steps, I leaned against the railing to rest. Sleep overtook me easily.

# Chapter 17

A barking dog somewhere close by awakened me. Momentarily, I was confused, forgetting where I was. Looking about to get my bearings hampered my ability to focus. I blinked several times, trying to clear my eyes, when I noticed a man approaching. Immediately, that made me uneasy, as there were no other houses nearby, nor did I notice any people at hand.

Shoulders somewhat hunched, kicking up dust with his shoes as they barely cleared the ground, he happened to look up and see me. Quickly I sized him up, as now he slowly came nearer, hesitating. "My God," I gasped under my breath. "What manner of creature is this?" His face was blackened; here and there you could see patches of white skin. The eyes were rimmed in black, his lips gray, giving him the look of an apparition. Instantly a fear came over me. Whether I shrieked or not, I cannot recall.

All I know is that whatever sound I made was enough to galvanize him to look at me for a brief instant, then in the next, he rushed toward me. Having dropped a pail or container of some kind, both arms extended, he stopped just short of grabbing my neck. I, in a split second, recoiled from what I had anticipated would be a death grip, hitting my head against the railing with such force that I sustained a gash to the right side of my forehead.

"My God, it's you, Ilija!" I screamed.

"And it's you, you whore! How did you find me?" he screamed back. "How did you find me?" he kept repeating as he pushed past me, leaping up the steps, throwing himself through the open door where I could see a woman just past it. She obviously had been in the house the whole time.

Heart pounding, dabbing at my bloodied forehead with my babushka, which had fallen off, I continued to sit on the steps. Totally shocked and unnerved, I couldn't collect my thoughts. All I heard in my mind was the question, what now? What now? It didn't take long to realize that Ilija was not going to accept me as his wife.

"But what is to become of me now?" I asked myself aloud.

Right about then a man appeared on the scene. Seeing me there, he was obviously puzzled, so he simply said, "Hello." Walking past me he walked up the steps and entered the house. The shouting from within could clearly be understood by me.

The woman was hysterical, asking repeatedly, "Is she your wife? What is she doing here? What are you going to do with her?"

Ilija's voice betrayed his own hysteria as he cursed and yelled, "Send her back, send her back." The only rational voice I heard was that of the man who had just arrived.

"Listen Ilija, you cannot send her back. Even I know that. Obviously, you are taken by surprise by her arrival, but she is here, and we have to find a place for her till we can decide what to do next," reasoned the man in a controlled yet loud voice.

More cursing—Ilija was beside him, yelling, "I never wanted her, never! But you know how it was. Hurry and marry and get it over with. I heard she had a child, a boy. He died. How do I know it was even mine? If I knew a *charatisa* I would order a spell to be cast upon her to get rid of her. I would pay anything."

At that, the man laughed. "Consider yourself fortunate to have left all that foolishness behind. A curse, a spell indeed, you are a silly man. Now get yourself together; we need to talk sensibly."

Suggesting that Ilija calm down only served to fire him up even more, as he then yelled, "I will kill her! It is the only way. I will. I will. The sooner the better. How dare she present herself as though she has a right to be here? She is as good as dead."

The man exploded in a torrent of strong, angry words, yelling, "You are not a man in my eyes. And while I'm bringing all of this up, what of your partner in crime, Jordan? For the longest time, after you left, it was believed that you left Sofia pregnant till she admitted that Jordan was responsible for abandoning her as you had abandoned Mara. No one has heard anything of Jordan's whereabouts here in America, but it could've been you just as well. At least you were married to Mara, but Sofia was left for the dogs of gossip to devour her. When Ivan married Sofia, we believed him to be a fine man, stepping forward to save Sofia, but it was later learned that her parents paid him to do so, practically impoverishing themselves. Sofia gave birth to a son, somewhat early; the child died. A story circulated that she had leapt from the hay loft onto the hard ground below, injuring the child. She never bore any other children.

"Have you no remorse? No shame? Women suffer greatly at the hands of men such as you. So, I tell you that your careless treatment of Mara now is no different than the abuse you left her subjected to at your parents' home. I condemn you as a self-ish man who thinks only of himself. I will do whatever I can to assist Mara. I do not need your permission. Further, I shall tell her that she can and should divorce you."

I frankly did not understand that statement. The man's state-ment that he would help me momentarily comforted me. Then the horrible dread; at what cost to me would this help come? I knew better than to trust any man. He would find that he was no match for me. All at once the shouting ended and the man emerged from the house. Briefly he stood on the porch before descending down the steps.

Still seated on the steps, my calm and commonsense restored, I smilingly looked up at him as he extended his hand to shake mine, introducing himself and saying, "I am David, a cousin of Stojan who lives here with his wife, Lena, and their three children. Ilija is just a boarder. No home, no wife or children—a poor excuse for a man. At this time all that I can offer you is this place here." And as he was speaking, he pulled me up and was steering me by one of my elbows to the back of the house. Pausing, he said,

"Wait a minute while I pull up this door." Stepping away, he grasped the handle of one of the twin doors, revealing steps going down to an area dug into the ground. I could see the dirt that was compacted into what could be called a floor. The smell that greeted my nostrils was of moldy, damp ground, and something rotting—I knew not what.

"Step down here. I will show you that this is a large place where a bed, stove, table, and chairs can make you comfortable for a while. Frankly I am ashamed to tell you that you have no choice at this time but to stay here," he said, looking away from me.

"And frankly I can say to you," I said, "that I am too fatigued and shocked to decline." Ruefully I added, "The dirt floors at home are better, and I see the tales of an abundance of good things in America are greatly exaggerated."

Hastily David left, saying, "I will bring your things to you; they are still next to the steps." Looking around the dank, dark place that I would call home, a feeling of deep despair settled over me. Maybe home over the ocean was not so bad after all.

"Who am I now?" I asked myself aloud. David's quick return interrupted my thoughts of self-pity. His voice had a hint of compassion and concern as he spoke. "Mara, this is shameful treatment for anyone, and you certainly do not deserve such cruel disregard for a woman so long abandoned by her husband. All I can say is, be patient. Somehow this will all work out. One thing is certain; you no longer have a husband. Sit up in the light and fresh air. I will return with something for you to sleep on, but most importantly, I will bring food, as I know you must be famished by now." With that he left.

I, taking his advice, did go out into the bright sunlight. Seating myself on the grass, I waited for David's return and again said aloud, "Somehow I shall endure. All I need is help from you, God. So just give me the strength to survive." For early October the weather was very pleasant—not yet cold. The sun felt good. It was energizing and soothing at the same time. David returned. He was struggling with a large roll tied up with rope.

"Step away from the door, Mara, so I don't knock you over with this." Carrying the roll down the steps, he dropped it on the dirt floor, whipped out a small pocketknife, cut the rope, and unrolled the thing he called a mattress.

"Again, I am ashamed to offer you this lumpy, not-so-clean thing to sleep on. There are a blanket, a pillow, and other things outside. I will bring them to you," he said. Returning in just minutes, he said, "The food will take a little longer. I have a friend preparing some food items and some milk. There is good water at the pump outside, so I will get you a pail of it. You can fetch all you need. The water is very cold and surprisingly good tasting."

"What is 'the pump?'" I asked.

"Ah, Mara, I forget. We didn't have any such thing at home." David was now smiling as he spoke. That smile eased me into a somewhat happier mood.

"Thank you, David. You are a kind man. Always I'll remember your help. Yes, you are truly a kind man," I said.

"Mara, I will do all I can to help you, but I do not want to overstep. I can only do what he allows. Please excuse me for that," David said apologetically.

Having heard what he had said to Ilija, I knew that he would not be consulting Ilija or asking his permission. I decided that David was a wise diplomat. "Mara, I am leaving now to get the food I promised. No one will bother you, at least not right now. They are all too preoccupied with themselves.

My pleasure is in seeing Ilija finally having to face you. He is practically a crazed idiot—so out of control. He deserves to suffer for what he has done to you. Although I frankly do not believe that the man is capable of feeling remorse or having any compassion for you. His nature is that of a brute—I see it whenever I visit here. I do not come often.

It is a strange household. If not for my cousin, Stojan, I would not bother with any of them. My cousin Stojan is a very indecisive, weak man who lives in a situation that he is not able to change. A few times I have attempted to talk to him about it. He is overwhelmed. Ilija dominates him and his wife, yet I would think that she would protest—at least for the benefit of the children.

Actually, they are all trapped. I myself am not a miner, and for that I thank God. My trade at home was carpentry. So, I find a good deal of work here. These mining camps are dismal, the houses always in need of repair. Everything is in a state of decay. You will see after a while. You will realize that the lives of these people are controlled by the owners of the mines. There's little opportunity to leave. So, year after year, the futility of life here crushes them," David said sadly.

All I could do was listen to his words, not comprehending what he was talking about. "Tell me, tell me, just exactly what is a mine?"

"Oh, Mara, my dear, surely you saw the condition of Ilija, all covered in black coal dust. The mine is underground, where the coal is dug out, brought to the surface, and finally sold. Coal is for making a fire in a stove to provide heat for cooking as well as heating the home. It is dangerous work. Many men have lost their lives. Men have difficulty breathing; they cough up black dust and blood, too, but they go every day. There is little work other than that.

God help me, I completely forgot about getting you that food. This situation here rankles me. I get carried away—forgive me," David hurriedly said, and then ran down the road.

*What was this America all about?* I puzzled. How could this be considered a life better than the one in our village? Suddenly the sun no longer felt warm.

My name was called out by David even before he came into sight. Excitedly he put down two large sacks spilling over with food. A large cabbage rolled out of one of the sacks. "Here is a bounty, I tell you, Mara. And better days are ahead for you, believe me, thanks to good friends that I have. They will provide whatever they can spare until I try to find you more assistance. Martin and his wife, Juliana, were so shocked to hear of your plight, they wanted to rush right over to meet you. This was not the right time, I told them. They did not need to get embroiled in the situation; there would be too much hostility."

Examination of the contents of the sacks revealed vegetables, fruit, flour, sugar, bread, a chunk of butter in a glass jar, a paper sack of fragrant ground coffee, and a small quantity of golden honey, also in a jar.

David stood, closely observing, saying, "This is so much more than I thought was in those sacks. They're kind people; incidentally they are not our people. They are English speaking, and I have no idea where they may have come from. Martin is not a miner either. He works for the railroad."

Sundown was upon us, so we hurriedly carried the sacks down into the cellar. David had also brought the bedding he earlier spoke of. helping me make up the mattress for sleeping, I could see a very different side of the man than I had originally judged him to be. David's manner was confident, not overbearing in any way. I could feel his compassion and sincerity, further revealing a man of goodness.

*Ah, Mara,* I admonished myself. *What meets the eye may not always be the truth. Just be grateful for what he offers. Repay him in kind, be accepting of his kindness, and remember to smile, yet be wary.*

"Tomorrow early, I will bring you a table and one or two chairs, and then I will get you a stove to cook on. That may take a day or so. Now I must say good night and sleep well," said David.

Sleep came easily. I was dead tired from the journey. Ilija's tirade and rejection had a very draining effect on me.

Awakening early, I knew it was daytime, as the sun's rays peeked in between the warped boards of the twin doors. I had not even undressed, having only removed my shoes. So, I was quickly ready to venture outdoors. Remnants of a light frost remained in the shaded areas. There was a certain smell to the vegetation and the soil. Well, Mother Earth performed her work all over the world in the same manner, I mused. It gave me comfort in finding something familiar in this new world.

Staying close to the back of the house, surveying the surrounding fields and houses, I felt more comfortable and confident each day.

Ilija never presented himself, just as I had anticipated, giving me a sense of power I had over him. Did he believe that I would crumble and head back to the old country? *Guess again, Ilija. You don't know my survival skills. I have endured much, and this too will test me but not defeat me.* Thoughts like that fired me up. I wanted to confront him in the house above, but I realized that I was regrouping—the same tactic a general would employ when an enemy threatened to decimate his troops. I heard of such tales in the old country. Power was to be my weapon. I would find a way out. I was sure that God would give me the strength.

Days turned into weeks. Soon two months had elapsed since my arrival. My daily activities, coming and going back into the cellar, along with my lonely strolls in the fenced yard had attracted the attention of neighbors close by, prompting them to help me in very unexpected ways. Women would cautiously approach the fence, gesturing to me to come closer, offering me food, sometimes an article of clothing and fresh milk. I reveled in their generosity, not quite able to understand such kindness. Soon we were conversing, or should I say attempting to do so, as each of us in fractured English and hand gestures managed to communicate well enough. Often there was laughter as the women corrected each other and me as well, trying to clarify the understanding of some words.

One day while the royal clan, as I referred to the occupants of the house above, was away, a couple came to the back of the fence calling out my name. The woman excitedly said something I interpreted to mean, "Husband fix fence; make gate." He had brought tools, setting them out. He took a segment of the wooden fence out, then replaced it with a sturdy gate with rusted, almost unmovable hinges and a latch. My first taste of freedom had come from people practically unknown to me.

Well-timed excursions beyond the yard to a neighbor's yard were so exhilarating I wanted to shout to Ilija and the clan, "Look at me; you can't stop me! I have allies who know my situation, and they too despise you." Believe it or not, the gate went unnoticed, or if it had been noticed, I heard no opposition to it.

These new people in my life gave me a strong sense of self-worth. Although I considered myself tough, self-doubt would creep in, dragging me back into the abusive, cruel years of the past. Resentment, hatred, and feelings of revenge could and often did take control of my life. These emotions festered within me so much so that to this day I am awed by the fact that I did not kill one of my persecutors. My fear of God's wrath, should I take a life, held me back. I am certain of that.

In just such a frame of mind, I sought vengeance. Ilija had to die. Oh, not by my hand, of course, but by God himself. While sitting in the darkened cellar, just one lonely candle casting a low light, I saw a shadow on the wall. I imagined it to be a sign of some kind from God himself. Studying the shadow more closely, I could see that it was the shadow of my night shirt hanging on a nail. How I managed to transform it in my mind as a divine signal I cannot say except to acknowledge a disregard for anything holy. It was in those few moments that I summoned God's help. Can you believe such a twisted, arrogant call on God to do my bidding? I did not care. All I wanted was Ilija dead.

By then I had learned the reality of the dangers of mines caving in. Stories my new friends shared with me of their loss of loved ones saddened me at the time of hearing of them. But now I wanted my own personal cave-in, and prayers for Ilija's death took over my life, undoubtedly spoiling what enjoyment was offered to me by caring friends. I never confided in anyone about my prayers. Perhaps because I realized that a mining accident always claimed the lives of more than one person. Once I started on this daily routine, it consumed me. Fearing that a lapse in my prayers would be a setback, I could hear myself mumbling evil words, all the while feeling justified.

My guilt about other men perishing was weighing upon me heavily. Almost daily, from an obscured vantage point, I watched the miners. The longer I watched them returning home, the more I was learning about them. They were brave men facing injury or death every day. Yet, like soldiers, they met the enemy. Each day of safe return was a victory. Often children rushed by to meet their fathers, calling out, "Daddy, Daddy!" practically throwing themselves at their fathers, carrying either their lunch pail or carrying their hat. The coal dust seemed to fall away amid their joy. Wives and others too would also start walking in the direction of the mine. Usually silent and glum faced, not until the last moment of the work shift did they relax, thankfully cheered that no calamity had marred that day. Yet here I was seeing the sad evidence of families living in fear, every day expecting the worst while I was praying for my husband's death.

One rather cold evening, I was exhausted from my relentless praying that had now become so obsessive and crippling. Preparing for bed early, I was debating the wisdom of leaving one section of the cellar door slightly ajar. I wedged a piece of firewood into the opening to keep the door from closing. Of course I knew it was an open invitation to the beasties of the night. *Oh, do it,* I convinced myself. *The air feels so good and refreshing.*

The beastie of that night was not one that I had even remotely considered. Sometime in the middle of the night, I fought the battle of my life. In the dark I could make out the form of a man; the smell of him was pungent. Strong arms pulled me out of bed and threw me onto the floor. Too frightened to scream, I summoned up Herculean strength as I kicked him away. Throwing himself on top of me, his hands tore at my night shirt—I knew his evil intent. A hard, closed fist slammed the side of my head, rendering me helpless to do further battle. The battle was lost, forever imprinted in my mind; his final act of humiliation was to spit in my face, followed by an evil laugh, "That's for you, whore."

After the rape I prayed for Ilija's demise almost nonstop throughout the day. "Hah!" I'd say out loud preceding each evil prayer, "That's for you, Ilija." I even made up songs, dark, evil songs. I felt no shame or remorse. Only the exhilaration of expecting a special event.

I lived in dread of a pregnancy. What would I do? How could I care for a child? The hole I lived in was so insulting, making me feel worthless and doomed. Ilija was living above me, ignoring me; not a crust of bread nor a drop of water had he ever offered.

I noticed vague changes in the way I felt. I skipped my monthly cycle. I realized I was pregnant. I stopped eating and drinking—it didn't seem to matter. Yet my mind was clear. It had to be.

I prayed for a son from the start. A son, perhaps, could help me, but a girl would be a curse. A girl in my European culture is worthless. All she would become would be a field hand, someone's enslaved wife, a beast of burden, and like myself she would be worthless. She would be without value, and without a proper dowry.

The people upstairs certainly took no notice of my condition. They never saw me.

The ladies of this special guild that had rallied around me became even more solicitous. The pity in their eyes conveyed their pain for me. I had shared with them Ilija's surprise attack. The child would represent forever a defeat, an unforgivable lapse in my watchfulness, a constant reminder that Ilija had prevailed.

The only thing that saved my sanity was the expectation of spring arriving, heralding the awakening of nature and the chance to plant seeds in a garden. How soon would I be able to lay on the soil, listening for some kind of life? I thought of my childhood friend, Tina. How I longed to see her again. I prayed to her. "I know you see my misery. Send me a sign you still care."

The heavenly cycles said spring had arrived. As soon as the ground began to thaw, I began clearing an area that would become my garden. I brought dirt in a pail into my place, smelling it and feeling its grit. I felt that it was fertile soil.

Upon hearing of my plan, David's enthusiasm was immediate. He brought me a shovel, a hoe, a rake, and finally seeds that I wanted. In spite of everything, the garden took me back to happier times. Thoughts of Tina were comforting. My newfound friends and neighbors marveled at my garden and that I did it all by myself. The garden provided bounty for the coming fall and winter months: corn and herbs to dry, cabbage for sauerkraut in a crock, green beans and tomatoes to put in glass jars. Some of the women showed me how to can vegetables. David brought me jars and lids.

Months slowly added up to the expected time of my child's birth. No calendar at hand, I did as we did back home. I calculated time as I made note of the cycles in the heavens. Stars don't lie.

*This is certainly another hot August day,* I said to myself. There had been so many hot August days. A sweat-soaked, loose-fitting gown clung to my sweaty, immense belly. "This would be a fine day for you, baby, to come out and give me some relief."

Conversations with my belly were commonplace. After all, inside was a person. The position of the sun told me it was just past noon, one o'clock, maybe.

About then I felt the beginnings of the skirmish that would take place in my body. *A baby's struggle to free itself of the chamber that had housed it must really be fierce,* I thought. *Some signal it gets from God, I'm sure, tells it when to commence fighting.* I was pacing, getting prepared for the final moments of my own battle. Freshly washed fabric, actually an old sheet torn into pieces of various sizes, was laid out on the bed. In the corner, a blanket, freshly washed, embraced the dirt floor where I planned to deliver. The dirt floor was swept clean. A thick layer of sweet-smelling dried grass lay beneath the blanket. Preparations had kept my mind focused on two things: first, the baby's immediate needs, and second, the continuing prayers for Ilija's demise.

The pacing stopped; a sudden pain in my lower back was all the signal I needed. Hastening to the birthing place, I slowly let my body down, first to my knees, then into a squatting position. The ease of my child's arrival was awesome—even easier than my son's birth in the potato field. Of course, the circumstances were so different. My first child was born in dread: knowing full well what its future would be like. This time, although I did not have much to offer a child, I knew it would have a better chance. How, I did not then know. All I did know was that there were enough people surrounding me who expressed an honest concern. Wrapping my baby in a blanket, I carried her to the bed. I severed the cord with a pair of scissors.

Imagine my delight—a girl. We lay down, she on top of me. After a brief resting period, I sat up, taking inventory of toes and fingers. They were all there, topping off tiny pink hands and feet. Her hair, lots of it, was black like mine. A tiny nose, rosy little lips, eyes bright, of a color as yet not to be classified. With baby in my arms, I looked skyward, past the cellar door, saying, "Yes, God, it must be two o'clock on a Sunday. A most special omen." I heard myself saying, "Thank you, God, for this child. I was prepared to hate her, you know that. You heard me. I beg your forgiveness. Thank you for this gift."

I took my child outside in the sunlight to look at her, noticing in shock that she did not look like Ilija, nor I, nor any of our family, nor like my dead baby boy. Her skin was too fair. I knew my daughter would be a problem to marry off to a good Serbian family.

Childbirth was not all that difficult. Yes, on rare occasions a woman in our own village would die, but I had no idea how many women died in the more modern surroundings of America.

Not until my daughter had her first child did I learn of the absolutely barbaric practices that women in labor were subjected to in America. In the first place was the idiocy of putting a woman about to deliver flat on her back. Then was the added incredible

117

insult of knocking her into oblivion with anesthesia, which was beyond my comprehension. I was shocked when my daughter, Milka, described her labor with forced anesthesia, and that she had delivered while in that state, unable to assist in a natural delivery, and found wounds on her infant's cheeks and forehead created by forceps designed to pull a baby, perhaps not ready yet to be born, into the world. The scars on my granddaughter are still there. Adding to that, the nurses and the doctor, when he finally visited her, strongly suggested that she not nurse her baby and that she could take pills to dry up her milk and substitute formula-filled bottles that often sickened the infant. This I could not understand. Gravity is nature's foolproof aid to an easier and natural delivery. My people, although backward in the ways of educated people, knew and obeyed the laws of nature.

While in labor, my daughter, Milka, overheard a shocking drama in an adjoining cubicle, as nurses were attempting to delay the birth of a baby by sitting on the woman's legs. "The doctor isn't here. He'll be furious if we don't hold up everything until he gets here."

The mother was screaming, "Stop! Stop!"

Truly a chamber of horrors. What happened to mother and child is anyone's guess. Think the worst that could possibly happen, and you could be right. God help us. Today natural childbirth, free of drugs, has replaced the anesthesia that caused many problems for the baby. Still, I hear that not much has been done to place a woman in a bed or chair designed to open up the birth canal by taking the pressure off the buttocks, facilitating an easier, more normal expulsion of the infant. Births in water seem practical but too showy for me, sort of like a staged drama, but then, what do I know?

# Chapter 18

Ilija lived on but was no longer a thorn in my side, which by the way, did not mean that I no longer wished him dead. To me he was already quite dead. Only once did he ask to see his child, as I walked in the tall wildflowers on the far side of the fenced property. His only reaction was a clearing of his throat as he touched her hand, then walked away. In my heart I knew it was only a matter of time. I had learned to be patient. Ilija would not bother us for too long.

Whistles at the coal mine were shrieking, sending a chill through me. A few minutes before I had felt a tremor beneath my feet as I was hanging diapers out to dry on the fence.

I knew right then that Ilija was no more. The whistles continued—turning my insides to cold stone. I felt damned. There was no joy, no jubilation that I had won, that my evil prayers had won. Shame, indescribable, filled my mind. Could I ever ask God for anything again? Damnation would surely follow me the rest of my days.

The certainty that others had perished with Ilija numbed me. I had put them there with my evil prayers. Pressing my hands to my ears would not shut out the whistles, now joined by the clanking church bells. Screaming parents, wives, and children raced down the roads and paths toward the mine. Bedlam. Chaos. Medical people converged on the scene as swarms of bodies wailing and calling out names in agonized voices surrounded the mine's opening. Black dust poured out, covering everything in sight.

My feet were cemented in place as I continued to stand in the yard. Finally, I moved toward the cellar to check on my child. To my amazement the whole interior was enveloped in a haze of dust. My baby was crying, her tears streaking her face as they mingled with the dust. Wiping her face clean, I proceeded to sit down and nurse her.

Her dark eyes seamed to search my face for something. Long after she had her fill of my milk, she remained awake, hardly stirring. And to this day, I swear that every now and then she would sigh deeply, and her eyes would mist. An eerie sense of being found out by my child chilled me—still does.

That day was forever engraved in my mind: March 17, 1925. My child was now six months old. Ilija was another casualty of a mine cave-in that claimed the lives of six other men at that time. I was surprised when I was actually asked to view his body as it lay in a plain, unadorned box in the living room of the house upstairs.

"You look different, Ilija." I silently moved my lips. "But one thing: You are clean. Not smelling like that night. Your face is peaceful, your hands still coal stained and callused, and I see that you lost a thumb somewhere along the road of your life. There are no visible marks on you, but your chest seems very flat. You are frail and defenseless now, Ilija. Maybe my prayers were exactly what you needed. I see now that your life has not been a happy one. Poor Ilija, oh, sure," I callously added.

If Ilija's passing affected anyone, I certainly was not aware. The family upstairs was back to its daily routine. As for myself, I was very restless. I wanted to leave that place. I had no money except for the balance of the ten-dollar bills David had handed me on three separate occasions.

When I tried to thank him, he would just abruptly turn away and leave.

A neighbor had taken me to the company store, and I bought stuff.

The ladies provided my baby with diapers. Hemmed squares of fabric, obviously remnants of a sheet, were plentiful and appreciated by me.

At this point I need to mention a most unexpected, and I could say mysterious, visit by an elderly African American woman who arrived as I hung out the diapers. A young man and she arrived in a really small, rickety wagon pulled by a large horse. She got down, held out a bundle, spoke a few words I did not understand, got back up into the wagon, and left. I was so stunned, first at the sight of such persons like the ones I saw in Cherbourg, France, and secondly, at the kindness of still another stranger. The bundle was a sheet wrapping up some baby clothes and a dress for me. She never returned. None of my neighbors who observed her recognized her or knew where she came from.

Believe me when I say that my early exposure to stories of the supernatural and the antics of our village witch, Crista, had left a residual stupefying effect on me. I half believed that she was not real. Why had she sought me out? Never being able to figure it out, I slowly decided to turn it over to God. But it was not until ten or so years later that I began to understand how He works. Later on, I'll explain.

My baby was in her eleventh month and not yet baptized. David volunteered to take us by rowboat to a church across a nearby lake where the baptism could be performed. I did not trust him, even though he offered to be Milka's godfather. *Rowboat indeed; no thank you,* I thought. I politely assured him that the ceremony was not needed at that time.

Fall in my new country came with such a feeling of sadness—a wasted summer. In the cranking down, as I called it, Mother Nature gathers in her powers as she prepares during the time of fall for all things to conserve life's forces for reemergence in the new cycle of spring.

Spring, oh, that time of Mother Earth's reawakening. Even in her quiet time, she was at work, I'm sure, but looking forward to her celebration of all things living: new leaves, grasses, sprouting seeds, waters freely flowing, released fragrances indescribable in their first subtle form, growing ever more delicious and intoxicating with each passing day. Then at a time only she knows, all changes as summer approaches. One's nostrils are treated to even greater pleasures. The maturing of fields planted with rain, the bounty of fruit in the trees, the grape-laden arbors, the flowers hosting bees and butterflies, dazzled one's eyes and senses. Those are my memories of my life in the old country. All the labor, fatigue, and worry about climatic conditions washed away as we gratefully thanked God for His grace. Once again reminded, I thanked God for my memories of the old country.

Unless you are one of us humans who worship Mother Earth, you can't feel the pain, the frustration, the anger of being denied the miracle of planting, tilling, and finally, the glory of harvesting. When I first arrived at Ilija's house, I was standing idly by as the ground went to waste. The royal family had planted not a single seed. There was ample ground in that fenced plot that would have yielded many vegetables and fragrant herbs. But instead, tall grasses and wildflowers of many colors filled the place. I was grateful for their beauty and the butterflies and bees that presented a continuing drama as they did their work. Nature provided them with such a wondrous place to do their work. I longed to do what I had always done: help Mother Earth give birth.

When I was finally able to plant a garden, I rejoiced. A fistful of earth, especially after a rain, smelled so good—it took me back. I'd rub it between my palms, loving the grittiness. Barefoot when the ground was softened by the rain, I would dig my toes into it, exposing earthworms, ants, and grubs all doing their assigned jobs. The marvel that never ceased to fill me with awe was God's perfect timetable for everything we saw and didn't see. Everything was in perfect concert. City life in America has not diminished my memory. It has only served to intensify it. *Ah,* I say, and *ah* again as I inhale those memories.

Responding to loud banging on the cellar door followed by David's bellowing voice, I rushed to see what was wrong.

"A letter came yesterday from a woman named Zeka Milich. She lives in Detroit, Michigan. You probably don't know where that is. The letter says she heard about Ilija's death and thinks you should come to see her. She says she can give you work and a place for you and your child to live. Also, there is some money in this letter, enough maybe to pay for a train ticket. What do you think?" David asked.

"Tell me again her name," I asked. "How does she know me? Why would she do such a thing?"

"There is no explanation here except she says she knew Ilija's family. The money is a loan, not a gift. You can pay her back when you start working for her. That's all I know." Having said that all in one breath, he took a deep lung-filling breath, and plopped himself down on my cellar steps.

"So," he asked again, "what do you think?"

What I thought was instantly clear: It was a way out.

# Chapter 19

The answer to David's question was manifested in my arrival at Zeka's home. From the first moment, I had serious doubts about my decision. As I sat at her kitchen table, holding my sleeping child, I noted the filth from ceiling to floor. Pots, stacks of them, dishes, all unwashed. Flies, doing what flies do. How soon would the maggots follow?

Zeka droned on and on and on, one fragmented sentence after another. "My dear," she kept saying, "I have a good establishment here. There are not many landladies up to the challenge of providing food and lodging for our brothers from the old country. Hard-working men that they are, they deserve a great deal of food, a bed, some place to play cards and smoke, and in general a place to relax and enjoy themselves. My wine is very good. We make it here. We can get fine whiskey too. That's why my place is preferred to others." She kept extolling the amenities, not once telling me what my duties would be. Yet she did not have to.

Our assigned room was actually a large closet jammed full of trunks, dirty clothes, and smelly men's work boots. I could organize this mess, I assured myself. Besides, I could open that window up high near the ceiling. Something to stand on would be needed to reach that window.

Actually, I did not stay long enough to organize the space or to open that window. Next came the appearance of an old man, fresh from work, but not fresh in any other way, as I had already smelled him before he stood in the doorway.

"Welcome, welcome, little widow. And of course greetings to your infant." His kind of eyes I had seen in my uncle's head, and my instincts told me to clear out. He continued, "Zeka told us about you. I had been looking forward to your coming. We need you here." He bared his teeth as he threw back his head, laughing gleefully. His teeth were stained brown, full of food, accompanied by a breath strong enough to knock over a stout horse. As his hand reached out to me, I tried to sidestep him, but not before a vice-like grip attached itself to a breast.

"Pig!" I screamed. "Is this the purpose I have been brought here for?" I spat in his face, and he backed off. I slammed the storeroom door shut. I seized my sleeping child, abandoning my belongings, and I was out the door, running. I headed down the sidewalk till I was out of breath. I just wanted to get out of sight of that cursed house, that den of sin. Emotions descended upon me. I was gasping for air. I was fearful of dropping my child, so I sat down on the bottom step leading to someone's porch. I could hear myself crying, yet I would not admit that the salt I tasted came from my eyes.

Fully out of control, my wailing attracted some people. Soon a small crowd stood around us, and I could hear the babbling of many voices. There was a great deal of hand waving and words I could not understand. I just did not care. Milka's bonnet was soaked with my tears. She still smiled—always smiled. Reaching up to my face, she said, "Mama," or something near that. Still I cried, now even more loudly, as my child's touch had just melted my heart. The tears became happy tears as I blew my nose on my babushka. A feeling of calm came over me. I could see the people more clearly. Questions, questions, I did not understand the language. Thank God I had enough presence of mind to say the word "Yugoslav." That momentarily silenced the group, and then someone said, "Oh," and took off running.

Moments later two men hurried in our direction. One of them was leading the other through the now larger throng of spectators. "Zdravo, gospodja," one of them said. "Kako si ti? Moje ime je Zlatan." God had sent an interpreter, and I will in turn interpret for you. "Good day, madam. How are you? My name is Zlatan." And may I add that the name means "golden one," as he was indeed.

I then answered many questions as to who I was and from where I had come, the circumstances of my husband's death, where I lived at present, and so many more questions. Some of the spectators had drifted off. No more excitement here obviously.

"Well, young woman," he said in our language, "you are fortunate to be the widow of a coal miner. You are entitled to money from the mine owners. We will need more specific information to obtain that money for you. Now it is more important for me to get you to a safe place where you and your child may stay for a few days. Then I will have the time needed to get all the information."

Before the day was over, Milka and I were in a very safe place. How those people, without phones, managed to contact all the right people, I cannot begin to imagine. We were in the home of a Red Cross lady who rose to the occasion of rescuing us.

In exactly three days, Zlatan presented himself, all smiles, just bursting with good news. In speaking to other coal miners' widows living close by, he learned that I could expect to receive about thirty dollars a month for myself and my child. "What's more," he explained," I will find you a place where you can live. I will advance you the money till your money comes in; that way you can get settled immediately."

Zlatan brought me to view a little house. It had three rooms: a kitchen, two bedrooms, and an outdoor bathroom shared with the flat next door. Zlatan had shown me a number of places; this one was the cleanest, and besides, the kitchen sink was bigger. But the most unbelievable thing about all of this was that every one of the houses I'd been in since I arrived in Detroit had running water. Oh, Holy God, what a miracle. I thanked God that he had gifted man with such a fine brain that could devise such astonishing things.

Furniture was needed. A table, two chairs, and a bed were donated by the woman next door. I didn't want to accept anything from a stranger, nor did I want to obligate myself. Worse yet, she could be a gossip who expected to spend time at my place. The woman's name was Ruth, a most difficult name for me to pronounce.

Ruth had five children, all grown. She was a very young grandmother. She and her husband, Paul, took me under their wings. They found me a used cookstove—it was enormous. It was a stove for cooking and also for heating. It could also be used as a coal- or wood-burning stove, or it could be hooked up to gas. When Ruth tried to explain to me the versatility of the stove, I just could not understand. So, she proceeded to explain that she could call the gas company so that I could use the stove more conveniently.

She said, "You just strike a match. I will show you how to be careful. Gas is easier for cooking. It costs a little more than using wood or coal."

When she mentioned money, I said, "No money."

Ruth replied, saying, "Then you will need coal or wood, which costs money too, but less. Once a week a man comes down the street selling coal and wood. We will show you how to buy some from him. There is a shed in the backyard to keep the coal or wood."

Okay, that was taken care of. Now I needed kitchen things: pots, pans, and dishes. Thank God there were window shades, such as they were: dark green, full of holes, very old, and very dusty.

"Curtains. You need curtains, Mara," said Ruth.

"What are curtains?" I asked.

"Something nice to fix up the windows and make them pretty," Ruth explained. Well, as it turned out, Ruth had more pleasure out of picking out the curtains at Schwartz's Department Store than I did. My concern was the money. Yet when the curtains were up, I marveled. How could people make these so beautiful?

One night, with Milka asleep, I sat in a rocker and studied the patterns. The streetlight outdoors highlighted the design of flowers and scrolling trails of vines, sending my eyes in search of faces. I had not tried to conjure up any in a long time. There were so many of them. I stopped after a while; I wanted to save some of them for another time. I was feeling quite happy that my new faces would not blow away or disappear. The patterns revealed birds and animals; whole scenes came to life as I leaned back in the rocker, spending many pleasant evenings. Half closing my eyelids, I sometimes fell asleep watching the curtains. The curtains are long gone but not the memories.

All of this went to my head. I was queen of my domain. What else could I want? Plenty of money—money left over each month; I lived very frugally. A place of my own. Pay the rent and no one sends you away. My lifestyle was wonderful: a widow with a child, taking care of herself with the exception of needing an interpreter from time to time. The new language was difficult, making me feel insecure and distrustful. I really worked hard at learning.

An occasional man from my country would try to call on me. I was insulted. What kind of woman did they take me for? I would order them off my porch. I never unlocked or opened my door. My reputation was not to be soiled by those worthless unemployed men. How did I know that about them? Well, of course I was suspicious of any man, especially the ones who were unshaven and dirty—you know, the slob type. After my experience with Zeka, I also suspected that she would put them up to bothering me. Why wouldn't I think that? Zeka, my own country woman, had given no thought to sullying my name. I hoped never to see her again. But wait, I'll tell you more about that later.

Milka was now almost two years old, my pride and joy. A neighbor man had constructed a gate for the porch. We, she and I, enjoyed the porch so much more with a safeguard that prevented an accidental tumble down the steps. Sundays were always the best. It was a time that I could observe families—fathers were at home, schoolchildren as well.

After church there was a great deal of socializing from one house to the next. My pleasure was in observing them and responding to greetings of hello, and there was also a greater opportunity to work on my English with so many people around.

Gradually, as I ventured out—not just to buy groceries—I was being treated to a new way of life. People greeted each other. Children played in the street as mothers watched. Evenings, like Sundays, brought the people out of their houses, where they gathered on the porches and steps, calling out to passersby and neighbors. Soon I was emulating them. Neighbor ladies wanted to hold my baby and to play with her. Oftentimes a gift of a crocheted bonnet or sweater was bestowed upon my little one.

Such generosity—such open-handed giving—was still alien to me, even when I recalled the kindness of the women in West Virginia. Suspicion seemed to lurk in my mind all the time. I wondered if there were hidden motives.

Ruth was my rescuer, as she taught me where to do my banking and pay the utility bills. Fortunately, I lived within walking distance of those places. When Ruth one day suggested that I take my child to a clinic for a medical checkup, I hesitated. There was no such facility in our neighborhood.

"How do I find this place?" I asked.

"Not to worry. You will find it so easy. I will write the address and the trolley you want to take. It is so easy, you will see," said Ruth.

I protested, "You know I can't read. Not one word."

"I will write it down. You will show it to the conductor. He will tell you where to get off. Then you show the paper to people where you are getting off. They will give you directions," said Ruth.

To tell you the truth, I looked forward to the challenge. With a small cloth sack I had sewn slung over my shoulder, baby in my arms, I stepped aboard the trolley as instructed by Ruth. The number on the trolley matched what Ruth had written.

The conductor read the piece of paper, saying, "Sit down in back of me. I will tell you when you are there."

And so it was, when I reached my destination. The clinic was staffed with people who treated us so kindly. They fussed over Milka. She was a beautiful child. They checked me out too.

"Take this letter to someone who reads English. They will explain when you should come back. Better yet, bring someone with you who speaks good English," advised a nurse.

Almost daily Ruth was pressed into service. She helped us willingly, kindly, as always. In spite of her obviously sincere friendship, I had this deep doubt and distrust. I was driving myself crazy wondering about hidden motives. Her eyes always looked at me directly, making it difficult for me to look away. I didn't like that; it seemed to me she could read my mind.

As time passed she could sense my awkward uneasiness as I averted my eyes. My body would stiffen; the tone of my voice became almost hostile. My awareness of this trait was slow. But Ruth persisted in what I sometimes felt was too much intrusion— a blessing in disguise I would someday appreciate. Time is always a factor in learning anything. After a while I felt a kinship with Ruth that I had never felt except with Tina in my village.

When my thoughts wandered back to my village, sorrow would grip my throat so painfully. *Our people are so pitifully ignorant,* I thought. *No one to teach them, to show them a better way to live.* I was well aware that peasant life imposed many limitations insofar as creature comforts were concerned. However, it was the hostility, the harsh words, swordlike, that cut deeply and repeatedly, that clung to my mind. Remembering that brought on guilt, especially when I was reveling in things like a clean, warm bed, clean clothes, enough food, and most of all, kind friends.

Hardly a day went by that I didn't ask God to forgive me for wanting Ilija to die. Through his death I acquired my financial good fortune. Most of the time I rationalized that I had committed no crime; Ilija was a cruel man. So somewhere between guilt and rationalization, Ilija's demise served us well, I decided.

Yes, my home was perfect. Even with cracked plaster, peeling paint, uneven, warped floorboards, hazy glass in some of the windows, and a shared outside toilet, it was yet a home better than anything in my village.

Wash days were easier than the ones in my village. A pair of wash tubs, a washboard, heated water in large buckets on the wood-burning stove—a most time-consuming chore, yet I was happy with it all. I bathed my baby in the kitchen sink—only as needed was the way I saw it. Sponge baths sufficed. My baby smelled clean and fresh. As for me, a bath was a major undertaking. When my child slept, I prepared for the chore. It took a lot of hot water to fill one of the washtubs to a point where I could submerge my bottom. With folded-up legs, I filled the tub like sardines in a can. What a luxury it was, nevertheless.

Shampooing my hair was a bimonthly event. Using the kitchen sink, ladling heated water from a large soup pot on the stove onto my tresses took a great deal of time. No shampoos, rinses, dryers, or such, yet admittedly, my hair was my crowning glory. It was always combed, fashioned into a pair of thick braids that I could style several ways. I was proud. My hair was uncut, never trimmed; it just grew and grew till it reached the floor as I sat in a kitchen chair combing it. In fact, it fell in folds on the floor. In my entire lifetime, my hair was never cut. Aging limited its growth, yet it was waist long until the end of my days.

# Chapter 20

Late one Sunday after Milka and I had gone inside the house, I heard a knock at my door. As was my careful habit, I always kept it locked. Peering through the curtains, I saw a well-groomed, finely dressed man, hand raised to knock again.

"What do you want?" I called out.

In our language he asked, "Are you Mara?"

And I countered with, "If I am, why do you ask?"

"Have no fear. If you are not secure in opening the door I understand. But I wish to speak to you."

"What about?" I asked. "I have nothing to give you."

"No, no dear lady. I am here on behalf of a respected friend of mine and to tell you briefly he seeks a wife. Word of your circumstances have circulated in the Yugoslav community," he smilingly said.

"A man—that is the last thing I desire. Say no more and leave. No offense, but I would not consider anyone," I declared.

Again he spoke patiently, politely. "Hear me out. Your reputation as a good, honorable woman interests my friend. He seeks a widow with up to three children. He has never been married, he earns a good living, he has no bad habits such as smoking or drinking, and he would be completely loyal to one woman."

"Such a virtuous man. How is it that he is not already married? Hah. There is something seriously wrong with him, I would say."

"Oh, no. The man has until recently lived in Pennsylvania with his brother, sister-in law, and their eight children. Jovo is his name. Incidentally, for many years he has devoted himself to financially helping his brother's family. He has decided to come here and to create a family of his own," said the man.

"A family! No, no. That is not for me. I do not desire to have more children, therefore, I cannot marry."

"Listen, Mara, I should probably not divulge something so personal about Jovo, but he cannot father children. That is why he seeks a widow with children. And may I emphasize that he is truly a good man. Perhaps you should consider meeting him next Sunday. I can arrange everything."

"No, no. Excuse me, I do not want to be rude, and please do not insist."

This had grown wearisome for me. It was too much to think about, so I just finally blurted out, "Next Sunday bring him by, but not to my house."

This statement sounded senseless even to me, so what must this man think? That I was stupid, of course. Puzzlement was etched on the man's face; he was silent. A dreadful, long pause followed. He seemed poised to walk away.

I spoke again. "What I mean to say is, could you walk past my house, on the other side of the street? I do not want my neighbors to get the idea that I am a woman of loose morals. Men are not invited to my home. That is a firm rule of mine, and I apologize for not opening my door, but it is my way."

Again with a smile, the man spoke. "Bravo, Mara. Jovo and I will do just as you say next Sunday afternoon about this same time." We agreed.

Again he spoke. "Before I leave, my name is Andria Dragicevich. My friend will be happy to learn that you have consented to see him."

Not until Andria left did I take notice of his appearance. Certainly, without my realizing it, it was the man's attire and manner of speaking that had allowed me to even speak to him. He was tall, nicely built, and an easy smile enhanced his good looks and believability. I think I blushed. Imagine that.

# Chapter 21

Slowly the week wore on. Thoughts about the coming of Sunday were alternately ones of regret that I had agreed to such a viewing and on the other hand feeling flattered that someone would think of me as a proper prospect for a wife.

Milka was fast asleep, thank goodness. How she slept through the sound of my pacing and muttering amazed me. I was peeking through the curtains, focusing on a single chosen spot where I felt I could best see this person. I spread some of the fullness of the curtains to one side to get a clearer view. I made sure that the window was still adequately covered. I did not want to appear eager. Fussing with the curtains highlighted my nervousness. I glanced in the direction of the clock—my God, it was almost time now. *So,* I advised myself, *pull up a chair, calm yourself, and get ready—you are not committed to anything, only a look.*

There they were, just a few houses away. Two men: one, Andria, the other, Jovo. "Ah," I spoke aloud, "he knows how to dress." Jovo wore a suit, pressed trousers, a white shirt, tie, hat, and polished shoes. I amazed myself for such a quick and thorough assessment of the man's appearance. *Oh, yes,* I said to myself. *He has a neat mustache.* At that moment, directly opposite my house, he turned slightly, raised his hat in a gesture, signifying some kind of greeting, I thought, and continued to walk briskly away.

My mind turned off as I sat for a moment, not stirring. My baby still slept, that is until I very loudly exclaimed, twice to be exact, "He is bald! What do I want with a bald man?" Milka awoke; I had frightened her. "Bald indeed," I said to her. Carrying her, I kept saying, "Bald, bald! He is bald!"

My fixation with his baldness confused even me. Certainly, he more than passed my expectations in appearance. I reasoned finally that I was merely looking for an excuse to drop the whole thing. Again a week passed. No word from Andria. That was good. Surely that meant that Jovo didn't think much of the idea either. Hah, no such luck. The very next Sunday, Andria presented himself at my gated porch. I had been enjoying the sights and sounds of my neighborhood. I was relaxed as Milka played nearby with a little five year old girl from across the street. Andria smiled approvingly. I sensed that he liked what he saw. My face flushed as I stammered, "Hello, Andria."

"Hello, Mara. This is a pleasure." He extended his hand, and we shook hands. I was more at ease now, asking him to join me on the porch. He took the other chair, crossed his long legs, and quietly waited for me to speak. I did not. He took the lead. "Did you happen to see us last Sunday? What was your impression of Jovo?"

At that point I invited Andria into my kitchen, as I felt we needed more privacy. "Well, I did see you and Jovo, of course. But I will be frank; I do not wish to waste words. He looked just fine, very fine, in fact, but a bald man?" I asked. At first Andria was trying to conceal a smile, but broke out into an uproarious laughter that went on and on until I was exasperated. Still laughing, I didn't think he could hear anything else I might have to say. Arising, he extended his hand again. I did not reciprocate. There would be no handshake, I angrily decided.

"Mara, I do not pretend to understand women, especially one I have just met, but surely you do not think that the man's brain is also gone? He is an intelligent man. But I will not pursue this. I will tell him that you reject the idea of marriage—is that correct?" he asked. Unfastening the latch on the gate meant a definite goodbye.

"Wait, Andrea. I am rude. Please forgive me. Perhaps I should meet him. Will you arrange it?" I asked hurriedly.

Once again, a Sunday. Sunday was a lucky day for me; Milka chose a Sunday to make her debut into my world. Well, I could not have dreamed just how well Andria would plan the meeting. An automobile pulled up. Out stepped Andria. Jovo disembarked from the back seat. Jovo stepped up to the front passenger door and opened it, assisting a woman to exit the car. Of course, I deduced immediately that she was Andria's wife. Oh my God, where was my housekeeping? The apple strudel I had baked that morning would definitely please them, I was sure. Until I worriedly realized that another woman would be the judge of that. Introductions were comfortable. We politely chatted as I served coffee and strudel at the kitchen table. I caught myself glancing at Jovo more than I should. I admonished myself. Andria spoke.

"Alice, come. Let's you and I take a walk and give Mara and Jovo an opportunity to talk by themselves. Can we take Milka with us?" I unhesitatingly agreed to my child going with them. This would be the first time she would be out of my sight.

I was shocked that I considered it all right, and somehow the gesture assured me that these people were trustworthy and safe to associate with. Perhaps it was the angelic face of Alice, paired with her genteel, soft voice as she spoke to Milka.

Jovo and I, sitting across from each other, quickly came to the subject at hand: marriage. He gave me the same facts that Andria already had. I was impressed with his devotion to his brother's family. The fact that he was born in a different region of Yugoslavia that fostered the education of children meant that he was a man capable of reading and writing. This coupled with his work record definitely set him apart from others who had come knocking on my door.

Many points about ourselves and our expectations were discussed in detail. The look on Jovo's face indicated to me that he was pleased; perhaps he was thinking that I would be a suitable candidate. But then perhaps he was considering others as well. As for me, I wavered between a yes and a no, thank you. I was relieved when he suggested that we take some time to think about things.

A week passed with no word from Andria till one unexpected evening he came by with Alice. "So, Mara, have you given serious thought to Jovo's proposal?"

"Proposal?" I knew of no proposal. But then again I may have closed my mind sometime during our talk. "Ah, yes, Andria, I would prefer to speak to Jovo personally one more time," I said.

"Good, good, Mara. If he agrees, next Sunday I will deliver him and return to pick him up at whatever time the two of you agree upon."

Hearing the closing of the car door, I went to the window to see if Jovo had arrived. Yes, there he was. The car left. He stepped inside, took off his hat, and asked, "Shall we sit at the kitchen table?"

"Of course, let us do that," I answered. We were nervous, eyes not meeting. I remember wiping the palms of my hands on my skirt; they literally dripped. After a long silence, I looked up. He was looking at me with his clear blue eyes.

"Jovo, I have done some serious thinking. You are aware that I, as a widow, receive a widow's pension. Well, I just found out a few days ago that my portion of the pension will end when I marry. My child's portion will continue till she is eighteen years of age. I have grown accustomed to the money. It is my security. I have not had to depend on anyone since the checks started coming. This is a sorrow to me, to give up the money."

Jovo spoke. "Yes, Mara, I do know. Marriage would end that. I have already given this thought. I believe that we could forgo marriage and live as a married pair. Who is to know? I am risking grossly insulting you by suggesting such a solution, but I do understand. The money is an important consideration. What if, once married, we should, God forbid, find that we are not suited partners? Being unmarried, you lose nothing, and I would leave. No further entanglements."

*Ha, ha,* I was thinking as Jovo spoke. Not only was he very intelligent, but he showed genuine concern for my child and me.

Without a moment's hesitation, I quickly said, "Done. The agreement to not marry suits me perfectly. We will not dishonor each other by making this public."

"Agreed," he said. "However, Andria and his wife need to know. I want to be honest with them. We can trust them to keep our secret."

Having resolved our future, and with Milka snugly tucked into her bed, asleep quickly, I was free to sort out all the arrangements and adjustments to cohabitating as an unmarried couple and the charade of a married pair. Jovo more than impressed me with his wisdom.

Yet it was his physical appearance that swayed me. The fringe of hair at the back of his head was neatly cut; his mustache was also neatly trimmed, curving into attractive upward tips at the ends. Not a hair was out of place. Blue-eyed and fair of complexion, unlike my somewhat darker skin, with work-hardened hands and clipped, clean fingernails—I took it all in. Was I losing my mind?

# Chapter 22

I wish that I could say that Jovo, my child, and I settled into comfortable living—I mean, comfortable with each other. My decision to live with Jovo so quickly had set off alarms in my mind. There were fears and doubts, the most alarming of which was that I had lost my mind. Money was not the motivation—I had my own. Certainly not passion, I held that to be a worthless, dangerous state of mind. So, what was it that propelled me into what could be the most reckless decision I had ever made?

Let's face it; I didn't trust this stranger. Were we safe, especially my child? What if he turned out to be a molester? He was no spring chicken; why had he remained single? Was he just putting up a good front? Whenever he left the house to go to his job, the barbershop, or to the grocery store, I braced myself for a no-show. Lord, my own husband abandoned me, why would this man not do the same?

Keeping Jovo on a short leash was annoying him, he said. Yet I held him at arms' length as well. My wifely duty, as I remember it, was not much. Fear of pregnancy, in spite of his assurances that he could not father a child, ate at me. I made myself unavailable—know what I mean? Jovo never complained, so instead of being reassured that he was a decent man, I had other suspicions. Were there a wife and children somewhere just waiting to claim him? Finally, Jovo spoke up.

"Mara, I know full well what your life has been, but you will have to leave it behind." It took me a long time to realize that helping my brother support his family of eight children was wearing me down. Being around the children was enjoyable, but my situation of being unable to have children of my own was on my mind more and more. So, I left the coal mines in Pennsylvania, moved here to Detroit, and found a job and a place to room. There I met Andria and Alice. Her mother ran a boarding house next door to their home, and what followed, you already know. If not for Andria, I would not have found you or your precious child. I will take an oath, here, now, again, and as often as you need to hear it. I will be loyal to the two of you until my death," said Jovo.

How could I have known that his proffered devotion would be tested by what happened to my child just a few weeks after that? Jovo was at work, it was a nice day, you know, springtime, and I was daydreaming of planting time in the old country. There was no place here to drop a seed anywhere. There was concrete all around. I could not understand why the good earth would be killed like that.

Well anyway, my child was in my arms as I was rocking her. She was fussy, real cranky, and hot. Cold water-soaked cloths on her head did not cool her down. Earlier that same day, I mentioned to Ruth that my baby was sick. She looked Milka over and said something like, "She really looks not so good," and backed off gingerly. She hurt my feelings, like my child was dirty or something. I was worried but didn't know what to do. Ruth left.

A knock on the door made me focus, as I had been crying about my baby. "Who is it?" I called out. I never opened the door just like that.

Ruth answered, "Mara, it is okay. Help is here for your child." Some help. Within a half hour or so, a lady dressed in what I then thought was special clothing, carrying a smallish bag, but not a suitcase, arrived. She looked my baby over, putting a little stick of some kind in her bottom—that was a thermometer, I learned later—and put a device in her ear, then still another on her chest. I remembered that second device and the doctor doing that to me when I got off the boat.

"How long sick?" Ruth asked. "This lady is a nurse. She wants to know."

"Three days," holding up three fingers, I repeated, "Three days." Everything is still crystal clear in my mind. Ruth was asking me for a blanket. It was evident that the nurse person was orchestrating everything.

Well, you guessed it, my girl was really sick, and off to the hospital she was taken. When it dawned on me that she was being torn from my arms. I thought I would lose my mind. My child was screaming, "Mama, Mama! No, No!" and holding her arms out to me. Ruth was restraining me. Believe me, I fought her.

"Baby very sick, Mara. Needs hospital. Let her go," said Ruth quite calmly. A car was waiting outside with a driver; they were gone. I was incoherent and shaking.

"This is the end of the world to me," I said to Ruth.

"No, Mara. We go to the hospital tomorrow—see the baby," said Ruth. Ruth had to be trusted, as she was my only hope. She sat with me, holding my hand, softly saying, "We'll be okay. You see tomorrow." Tomorrow was a long way off.

The moment Jovo stepped through the door, he knew something was wrong. How he made any sense of what Ruth and I were babbling about, I don't know. Anyway, he thanked Ruth, saw her to the door, then pulled up a chair and sat down next to me.

"Okay, tomorrow we will go to the hospital to see Milka. Don't worry; we'll see what the problem is. I will stay home from work, so we can go together," he calmly said. Going to the hospital was the easy part. But to see the child was impossible.

Ruth came along, thank God; we needed her. There was a young girl in the office who happened to speak German, making it easier for Ruth to communicate with her. The girl conferred with the doctor for a while. She was nodding the whole time. I was certain the news was bad, and it was. Ruth's face was stoic.

The doctor said to us: "Your daughter has scarlet fever, and she will have to be in the hospital in a quarantine ward with other children who have the same illness. You will not be able to see her for quite a while, but when you come here, and you can come whenever you want, we will tell you how she is."

"What is quarantine?" I asked, fearing the answer.

"It means being separated from healthy people so they will not get sick too. It is a protection for her and us," explained the doctor.

Jovo reassured me that he had heard of such quarantines, and that they were good.

"Let's go home," he said. "We'll come back tomorrow."

I was calmer now, accepting what I had to, feeling comfortable in Jovo's presence. The days dragged on. The visits to the hospital were difficult. When would I see my child? After two weeks and still no visit with my child, Jovo had a suggestion.

He explained, "Next Sunday we will go to the hospital. When we get there, I will ask someone if we can see Milka through a window. You know, bring her to the window so she can see us, and we will see her."

On that Sunday I sat waiting for Jovo in a large room. There were many other people there. As he walked confidently toward me, I knew that he had accomplished his mission.

"It will be on the second floor—the corner window on the north side of the building. Let's go," he excitedly said.

That was fine, but I could not bear to let her see me. I was sure she would be upset. As we rounded the corner we were close to some pillars at the side of the entrance.

I said to Jovo, "You wave at her; I will peek from behind the pillar so she won't see me, but I should be able to see her."

"That's good," said Jovo. "Quick, hide." There she was in a nurse's arms. She was smiling, not crying. She responded to Jovo's waving of his hand. My heart did a dance, and I started to cry. Soon the nurse turned away; they were gone. Two important things had just happened: Jovo more than proved that I could lean on him, and best yet, my child had bonded with him. I can say now that they loved each other, and it was a strong love that lasted until his death.

And so, it continued, week after week, and I was losing my mind bit by bit, still separated from my child. What was going on now? Jovo and I were preparing ourselves for something, but we knew not for what. We each had our private thoughts, never quite saying aloud what our fears were.

Almost a month had passed; try to imagine what we felt.

The language barrier rendered us helpless. We depended on Ruth's translations. Ruth's own fractured English was not putting us at ease at all. The young woman who originally had spoken to Ruth in their language added to our anxiety, as she was no longer there.

On a Sunday morning, there was a knock on our door. Our response was immediate. We could see a car outside with a driver and a nurse. Was Milka being returned to us?

It was not the same nurse who took her away, but we were overjoyed when she said, "You will be taken to the hospital."

The trip to the hospital was not putting me at ease at all. So many questions to ask, and I was unable to ask a single one. Jovo had asked Ruth to accompany us. The pair up front chatted, once in a while giving us a smile. Smiles like that I didn't trust.

Finally, we were there in an office. A ruddy-cheeked, short man in white greeted us, asking us to sit down. Doom-doom-doom. I knew it. I knew it, and so did Jovo. He gripped my hand so hard it hurt. Oh God, I thought, he is as afraid as I am. Milka had been a very sick child. After the scarlet fever, she had another problem.

The doctor said, "We had to operate; it could not be avoided. But she has now recovered and can go home." He stood up to leave. I was full of questions, so I ordered him to sit down, and he did so. I didn't realize or remember till later that I felt I was facing a lying enemy.

I instructed Ruth to say for me, "Everything you have said tells me nothing that satisfies me. Are you telling me everything? Tell me now before I lose my mind." Ruth tried to translate, stumbling over words, half crying herself. Later Jovo told me that when I was ordering the man to sit down, he had signaled to someone with his raised hand, bringing two men to the area immediately.

Out of nowhere another man presented himself, saying, "My name is Dragomir, and I will do all I can to help you." He sat down with us in an alcove, speaking clearly and sympathetically. I thank him still today. We shared a language; he too was from the old country.

"You need to be prepared to see your child, and you need to know that the operation was absolutely necessary. She has bandages on the left side of her neck. You will take her home today, but you must return in a week to get the bandages off. Keep her quiet, give her plenty of food that she likes and lots of milk, and she must not disturb the bandages. Keep her in your bed at night so you can watch her more carefully. Now I will take you to where she is waiting for you," he said with a gesture to follow him.

Miles of corridors, this way and that, until finally we stood in front of an open door, and there she was. A sad, pale, thinner Milka—very quiet—we couldn't really be sure if she knew us. Dragomir assured us the medicine she was given calmed her down, stopping any pain she might have. "Here, take these pills with you. I will tell you how to use them," he said.

Yes, the child appeared to be drowsy, but why did she not know us? To me, that was a bad omen.

Jovo picked up on my reaction, calmly saying, "She will wake up when we get home." We were put in a taxi for the trip home. My child stirred in my arms, looking up at me, and weakly smiled and said twice, "Mama, Mama." Again she lapsed into sleepiness. Jovo and I took turns watching her as she slept, sitting on the side of the bed. We watched her every move, hoping she would awake and speak to us.

Sometime later the child awoke very clear headed and hungry. Thank God I had cooked the traditional chicken soup, a cure for all ailments. Jovo had gone to the grocery store, buying even more of the necessary ingredients for more soup.

We didn't know it then, but Jovo had just started a tradition that would survive for at least a decade. He had purchased a small layer cake covered in chocolate. After we had eaten, he brought out the cake, which he had kept hidden until that moment. Believe it or not, I had never before seen a chocolate cake. Our baking in the old country was made up of breads and some yeast-risen sweetened loaves, usually made at Christmas and Easter time. The cake was so tasty we ate it all up. We had such a fine time, especially the child. "More, more," she kept begging.

From then on there was always chocolate cake in the house. We would not gobble it all up in one night as we had the first time. I carefully doled out, the biggest portion to Milka. It lasted several days. Chocolate cake and cold milk at bedtime was truly established as a family tradition.

Milka was oblivious of the bandages, mainly because I had put a little piece of colorful fabric over it; she liked that. I, however, could not get the bandages out of my mind. What was under them? They had developed a faint disagreeable smell. I feared that smell. I feared everything. Jovo and I purposely avoided any reference to the operation, the hospital, the bandages, or what might come next. This stranger, this man, this sainted Jovo, was becoming someone I could count on. He had more than proven himself. He was indeed a family man.

Ruth's husband, Paul, had offered to drive us to the hospital for the bandage removal appointment. We were grateful. Once there, a doctor greeted us then sent us to a small room with all that equipment. You know, examining table, bottles of this and that. I felt very uncomfortable in that setting. The doctor returned, introduced himself, and took Milka from Jovo's lap, putting her on the table, all the while talking to her in a most soothing manner. As he was removing the bandages, a nurse came in. She introduced herself, then began to assist the doctor.

I was cringing. Would this hurt? And when could I see whatever was there? The child was sitting on the table at such an angle that the affected side of her neck was away from us. Watching the proceedings like a hawk, I was comforted by the fact that Milka was not fussing at all. But when I saw the expression on the faces of the two medical people, I knew. Something was dreadfully wrong.

The nurse spoke first. "As you know, your child was very sick, and the operation was necessary. The problem is gone now, but she has some swelling and redness, but not bad. Otherwise, she is fine."

My mind screamed, *Let me see, let me see!* What I saw was horrible. For a mother, a scraped knee or elbow is awful. What I saw was horrifyingly unbelievable. Not only was there swelling and redness, but the trail of a knife had left crisscrossed cuts that were not clean, but rather it looked more like torn flesh or a horrible burn. God, I almost fainted.

Jovo studied me, took a quick look, and said to Milka, "There you are, all better. Now we can go home."

What I wanted to do was to scream obscenities at whoever had done this to my child. I remained calm. I don't know how I managed it, but I did not want to frighten my child. Calmly

I asked, "Tell me, people, what was wrong here? And what did the operation fix?"

"Well," the operating doctor told us, "the scarlet fever went into the glands. They had to be removed." This turned out to be not true. Tuberculosis had settled in the lymph glands of Milka's neck. Glands had to be explained to me.

*Explain to me,* I said to myself, *how my child will live with this horrible disfigurement.*

Milka made a full recovery, but I did not. Whenever I saw that unbelievable scar, I cringed. Bathing her, combing her hair, or tending to her in any way, if it was near her neck, I choked up. It was so bad to look at.

The worst of the aftermath was stupid people staring, or worse yet, asking, "What is that?" My child was happily oblivious. I guess if she could not see it, there was no problem.

It is a wonder I did not drive my child crazy as I searched out people who could "fix it." Of course, plastic surgery was as yet an unknown skill. As she grew older—nine and ten and older—my paranoia about the scar grew. The big question to myself was, "Who will want a disfigured girl?" It was killing me.

A faith healer had set up a huge tent that attracted hundreds of sick people seeking a miraculous cure. Well, don't you know, I decided that I had to take my child there for a healing, you know, to take the scar away. I spoke to Jovo about it.

He said, "Do what you want. I don't want any part of it." He was not patient with me on that point. "Why do you insist on the unreality of such a trick, for it is a trick? This healer is a charlatan, out to deceive, take money, and give false hope. Most of all, you keep talking of the scar as though it is shameful. It is what it is. Milka never gets upset about it. It is a part of life." He turned to leave, delivering one last remark. "You see trouble where there is none. Such a waste."

*Hah,* I said to myself. *He is not a mother, neither is he a father.* Later I was ashamed of myself for having thought that. Jovo Djakovich was more of a father to her than Ilija ever could have been. He was a father in every sense of the word, a true, loving, caring father till he died at the age of seventy-five.

During those early weeks, while my child was still in the hospital, something quite upsetting happened. I didn't make the discovery immediately that someone had robbed me of fifty dollars in United States gold coins. At that time America still had gold money. Nothing had been disturbed that you could see, until I needed to get something out of my locked trunk. The lock looked funny. Then I found out about the theft.

Immediately I suspected Zeka, thinking that she didn't do it herself, but rather that she had an accomplice. I was sure she had decided to get even with me for leaving her place. I was positive that she was behind the theft, even though I had long ago repaid her for the train fare from West Virginia.

Fifty dollars was a good bit of money in 1926. It was money I had saved before Jovo and I got together. I saw no need to tell him what happened. Shame that I had not mentioned to him that I had the money was gnawing at me. He would never ask about my finances. He was much too fine a gentleman; however, it was my secret. I guess I was still not trusting him enough. If he left us, I had a little nest egg.

# Chapter 23

*Y*es, Jovo had proven himself once again, having brought my child and myself through a very traumatic health situation with his strength and his commitment to us. Throughout the years he enriched our lives, always finding ways to introduce us to books, poetry, and newspapers, to keep us informed of all manner of things. So, his announcement one day was perfectly normal.

"Mara, it is time for you to learn to read and write in our language."

"No," I protested. "I could never learn."

"But you will try, and I guarantee that you will succeed," Jovo encouragingly said.

Jovo was an educated man. The first four letters of his last name, "Djak," denote a connection to student or teacher. So, it was natural for him to bring education to us.

Before long the mailman delivered two books used in primary grades in schools located in Belgrade, Yugoslavia. He had already purchased a large-sized chalkboard, having kept it hidden in the woodshed.

Our kitchen became a school room. The teacher patiently instructed, asking me to write on the board as he called out letters of the alphabet. Simple words at first, followed in time by sentences increased my knowledge of the written language. Surprise, surprise, my child instantly became an eager, hungry-to-learn student as well. As is often the case, young children learn quickly. Soon she had advanced ahead of me. I was pleased, as she was only five years old at that time. As Jovo was teaching us to read and write in our native language, I became aware of new words foreign to our simple village vocabulary.

Milka spoke softly, shyly, as she read to us one day. For whatever reason, I began to find fault with the way she spoke. In an effort to put an end to what I judged to be a slow, "mealy mouthed" tone, I declared, "You must speak the words clearly, decisively, as though cutting off heads with a sword," all the while gesturing in a fashion akin to that—cutting off heads with a sword. The result I got was Milka running to another part of our small apartment and hiding.

Jovo was appalled. "You, Mara, are no longer living under the sword. Do not frighten the child." His voice was stern, his look disapproving, which was caution enough for me not to do it again.

My education was not complete. I thought I read well. Translating symbols on paper to words was always astonishing to me. One day Jovo announced, "Mara, you are now ready to attend night school. It is for people young or old who are interested in learning English."

Definitely I knew better than to protest. Notebook and pencil in hand, I presented myself one evening. Looking about, I did not see a single familiar face. *That is good,* I thought. *No one I know will see how stupid I am.*

English letters and their sounds, especially the vowels, were multiple in nature and difficult to learn. Milka was faced with the same challenge when she entered public school. Many thanks to our landlady's daughter, Sofie, who patiently helped us to master the differences.

Jovo continued to grow and grow in my appreciation of what he offered my child and me. He had a gentlemanly and scholarly demeanor and wisdom in teaching us so many things not found in books. By his example rather than any word, we learned much.

Manners were high on his list of things to know. My exposure in the old country to such a notion was limited. After all, there were so few niceties in our daily lives, I reasoned. Just being aware of another person so as not to hurt or demean by word or deed became a new way of life. Through Jovo I discovered the power of a compliment. He showered us with them.

Jovo was so aware of and appreciative of my contribution to creating a good life together. Countless times, sitting down to a meal, any meal, he would say, "Mara, you have prepared a meal fit for a king."

My reply, always the same, spoken with great dignity, was, "It is easy to prepare when the master provides."

Many times it was an evening meal of hard-boiled eggs accompanied by a lettuce-only salad. One of my specialties was a soup of boiled chicken feet filled out with anything in the pantry, more often than not potatoes, perhaps a carrot or two, a handful of beans, lentils, and a companion of freshly baked cornbread.

Do you know how much actual meat can be found on the foot of a chicken? Or that the foot of a chicken is that part of the leg between the drumstick and the foot and includes the actual appendage? The feet and the leg were first scalded in boiling water to facilitate the removal of a tough outer skin. Then the talons were cut off. The very center of the underside—I call it the ball of the foot—was where the bulk of the meat was found. It was small, perhaps the size of a hazelnut. The rest of the meat was comprised of sinew and tendons, yet if cooked long enough, it provided some nearly undetectable flavor. By the time you added whatever you had, it was filling—almost. I am not boasting or looking for sympathy, but as a woman fortunate enough to have a man and a child, I made certain that they, the working man and the young child, had enough to eat. What I am saying is that many a time I ate very little, making sure they were not hungry.

Jovo often asked, "Are you not well? You have eaten so little."

My standard reply: "Oh, I have a bad habit of sampling too much in the kitchen." At this point I need to mention that chicken's feet were purchased at the local meat market. A pound of those soup makers cost a nickel.

Earlier I told you about my fascination with fabric. Can you possibly imagine my awe at finding stores selling so many kinds of fabrics? Most amazing to me was the fine weave, providing softness. There were colors, colors, colors—amazing. Patterns were both imprinted and woven into the fabric. The fabric widths were wide enough to make bedsheets.

Our looms were only capable of very narrow weaving.

Towels! Imagine a fabric of tiny loops meant for water absorption. Laces, machine-made, threads for sewing and embroidery— how crudely I had embroidered at home. Now I was learning fancy stitchery, with silk threads yet.

Whatever I created, whether embroidered or crocheted or knitted or sewn, Jovo would never fail to compliment my work. He would carefully examine everything, commenting on the fine quality of workmanship. What a man.

# Chapter 24

Years of subjecting Jovo to tests of his commitment and loyalty never seemed to satisfy me. No matter what he did, there was always some kind of doubt. Could I finally trust him? I managed to forget the horrible hospital drama when he steadfastly stood beside me. Whether I was aware of what I was doing in those days, I don't know.

Now I realize that his life with me was difficult to say the least. His acceptance of my behavior, whatever personal feelings he might have felt on the inside, I simply regarded as being passive and somewhat weak. His acceptance of my attitudes and moods was a demonstration of his strength, his commitment to us as a family man. His personal strength was much more important to him than engaging in some confrontation with me.

Did I know that? Of course not. So, our lives as a family continued to be a complex, convoluted charade. Jovo, Mara, and Milka were an ideal family admired by "our" people. At church, weddings, christenings, and funerals, we presented a solid family picture: a married couple with a child. We had a small circle of very close friends who also admired us and even complimented us. That image was the one presented to "our" people. The other image was blurred and cloaked in deception wherever we moved, and we moved frequently.

My paranoia about being discovered as a widow on a miner's pension while cohabiting with a man who legally would be classified as a common-law husband cost my family a great deal. Only in my older years did I even occasionally want to think about it, much less admit the damage I had done to us. Money took precedence over everything.

Each new location we moved to was checked out by me beforehand. If the neighborhood had children, I went back to determine just which houses they lived in. I would never select a house in close proximity to children close to my child's age. I was determined to control the number of children who would seek out my child to play with. Also, I didn't want their mothers to become friendly—what I could call nosey.

Milka was isolated, kept from other children as much as possible. She was not allowed to go to a neighbor's house to play nor did I allow children to come to our place. She devised games to keep herself occupied; there were many hours spent playing office with discarded letters, envelopes, bent paper clips, stubs of pencils—all retrieved from the waste baskets that Jovo emptied as he cleaned the offices where he worked as a janitor.

His company, as he proudly referred to it, was family owned. The employees were well treated, like a family; the Holley Carburetor Company was known for that. Magazines with tattered covers were a staple as well. She had few toys. I deemed them useless and expensive. Paper cut-out dolls were cheap; I grudgingly bought those anyway. The paper dolls survived years of playtime—always carefully put away in a shoe box.

Of course, her most enjoyable activity was to drive me crazy with her constant questions about my life as a little girl.

# Chapter 25

A moronic plan devised by me alone to conceal the true identity of Jovo and the role he played in a loosely structured family unit was difficult to keep straight. Carefully I coached Milka, should anyone inquire, that Jovo would be referred to as an uncle or a boarder, as a situation might demand. Her confusion was exasperating to me. I didn't explain the reasons for all that subterfuge. The less she knew the better, of course.

At home she called him "Cheecha," meaning "uncle." When with "our" people, he was Papa. Craziness ruled my world, ruined my child's sense of security, identity, and belief in trust, and humiliated Jovo. I didn't give a thought to any of that. Each passing year reinforced my "good judgment" of what was best for us.

On occasion Milka would report that she overheard some neighbor women discussing our family structure. This was enough to set me on another quest for a different apartment. How stupid did I think people were? Our arrangement was very transparent. Of course, I felt that gossiping neighbors were the wrong doers.

After all, they were deliberately mean-spirited, knowing full well that it was hurtful to my child.

All this was accepted by Jovo. Not because there would be any monetary gain for him in my continued pension checks; he made it clear that he did not want that money mingled with his earnings. So, I had a separate savings account.

On more than one occasion I heard Milka say so sadly, "Cheecha, Cheecha, when are you going to be mine, just my Papa?"

He answered, "I am yours. I'll always be yours for all my life and beyond."

The beyond? I never said anything about that statement. How could I know it would be true? Yes, true. You see, Milka has never stopped mentioning him, even after his death.

She will say, "Papa is in another dimension, but he still loves me and looks after me."

She has built a mental shrine to her Papa. Her two older children were not too young to remember "Deda," meaning "grandfather," while the two younger children, born after Jovo's death, know him intimately also. They know all about him, from beginning to end.

Jovo Djakovich is known to countless people who have heard of his love and goodness. Friends and perfect strangers know of his wisdom, his dedication to us, and his encouragement in all that he sought to do; his love and memory live on.

Mainly Milka tells that he saved her sanity. Boy, today everyone talks so openly and freely about everything. That comment was meant to let them know that I was a difficult mother, and that her wonderful Papa made things better. Well, he did. But I didn't see it that way at all.

There was no value in coddling. Can you believe I thought kind, thoughtful, loving treatment was coddling? Where else, from whom else, could she have gained the qualities that made her a better mother than I was? Her dozens of friends are testimony to the fact that she knows how to be a friend as Jovo was. I was not friend material, ever.

Hiding and moving was the way the game was played, keeping one step ahead of any coal mine investigators. My panic was increased every time I visited two different widows, also from my country, living with men—one of them even having children by her man. Why I visited them is still a mystery to me. All I remember is asking them a lot of questions and then coming home with a killer headache. After each of these visits, my paranoia about being discovered called for new tactics. Of course, moving was one tactic, but you can't keep yanking your child out of school. So plans were made and altered all depending on the degree of paranoia I was experiencing.

There I was, the man in my life worth more than any money on earth, yet I couldn't see it. Going to church or any function that the three of us would attend together was spoiled by sneaking around, trying to confuse neighbors, who could readily see what a joke it was. It was obvious to everyone but me, the mastermind.

The routine called for an early departure by Jovo through the shed, the dusty alleyways, and across vacant lots, to catch a trolley to some transfer point, where he would wait for us to join him. My daughter and I made much of greeting neighbors as we walked down the sidewalks to the trolley stop. Some joke it was.

This wonderful man had wordlessly given me permission to humiliate him. Jovo dressed for church or a visit to friends and was always impeccably attired. He was always impeccably dressed in a custom- tailored suit, a fine white shirt, a tie, an Adams hat— or was it the Stetson brand? I am not sure—and his shoes were the final statement of a well-put-together man. His shoes were always polished, no frayed laces or run-down heels. Milka and he polished his shoes as he taught her the finer points of a shine.

Jovo's high standards for the appearance of a man's shoes were woven into a story he told Milka about the proud, showy peacock and his glorious feathers. The peacock's feathers were diminished by his very ordinary, unattractive feet.

He would be there, looking at the shop windows; Milka would approach him quietly, waiting to be acknowledged.

Softly she would call out, "Cheecha," and then she would correct herself and say, "Papa." Jovo always tipped his hat, hand extended. Milka and Papa were always reunited, holding hands tightly. I was the outsider. Often seeing them like that, I could not suppress the pain deep inside of me. As a child, I never had anything like that. Feeling resentment helped to dispel the pain.

Sometimes I allowed my memories to rekindle something of what I felt when I was with Tina. Lord, Lord. At that time, considering the clandestine nature of our relationship, I must have suppressed my deeper feelings for Tina. I feel the loss even now.

Jovo worked long hours as a janitor and general handyman. He took two trolleys to get to the distant factory where he proudly did his work. I recollect my first impression of him as I peeked through those lace curtains. It was his attention to his appearance, his pride in how he looked, which was his benchmark.

His work clothes were never really soiled. There was no grease or stain of any kind, except for patches of salt from sweating. Each day, in addition to carrying his lunch pail, he packed a paper sack with a change of shirt and pants. Why? He did not wish to offend anyone on the crowded trolley. He washed up before donning the extra set of clothes.

I paid special attention to his work clothes. We could not afford frequent replacement, so the first sign of wear was carefully reinforced with stitching or near-invisible patches. Buttons were always secured. I reversed the collars when they became frayed. No sewing machine—I did everything by hand.

Jovo always complimented me on the starched shirt and pants, which were carefully ironed. He wore them proudly. Milka's first lessons in ironing, when she was about seven or eight years old, were centered on Jovo's work clothes. Jovo, at my request, built a sturdy rectangular stool for her to stand on so she could reach the ironing board. It was handy at the kitchen sink as well. Milka inherited the stool, and I wouldn't be surprised if she still has it.

# Chapter 26

That stranger knocking on my door that fateful day in April 1926, changed my life and that of my child. Throughout the years I treasured with gratitude that man, Andria, who introduced me to Jovo.

His wife, Alice, and their four children filled out my life. I can't say that I ever trusted Alice's mother, who had been Jovo's landlady. How wrong and foolish I was to think that Jovo would be lured away by a former landlady. Besides, she had a husband. Andria and his family were at that point in time living with her. Another married daughter, her spouse, and two very young children also lived in the same house.

My impression of the woman was that she possessed a certain regal quality. Obviously, this could be a threat to me, I thought. All her family called her Majka (pronounced my ka). *How does she rate such a title?* I asked myself obsessively. Majka certainly translated into "mother" or "grandmother." So as far as I was concerned, this gave her a superior, revered grandmother status.

After all, she was a grandmother a few times over. So why was she not referred as "Baba" or "Baka," as was customary in our language? My decision to be called Majka, should I ever become a grandmother, was set in stone.

Andria, Alice, and their children visited quite regularly. Neither family having a telephone meant drop-in visits. This was never an inconvenience. I had learned their routine quite well. A Friday evening was really good for us. They had school-age children, and my child had also started school. We adults stayed up late. The kids, one by one, would drop off to sleep in a chair or sofa, on pillows on the floor, and such. In anticipation of these visits, I baked some kolach, a sweet yeast dough roll filled with ground walnuts. There was coffee or tea, milk for the children, and also some homemade wine for the adults. Those were wonderful times.

On Sundays after church, Jovo, Milka, and I would travel to Andria's place by trolley. It took two transfers to reach their home. We did this about once a month. Andria worked for the Ford Motor Company, so of course he owned an automobile. We always marveled at such a luxury in spite of a large family with financial demands. As an employee, Andria said he was eligible for a generous discount.

Well, sometime during the height of the depression, I cannot recall exactly what year it was, Andria and Alice turned to us for help. They arrived one midweek evening without their children. I asked Milka to amuse herself in her bedroom. At evening's end, we shook hands. Andria and Alice thanked Jovo and me, leaving in a most solemn manner. Jovo and I had a brief conversation, and then decided to tell Milka what had occurred.

Andria was in financial difficulties. His home was facing mortgage foreclosure, needing seven hundred dollars to save it from legal action. Jovo and I did not hesitate for a moment. Our regard for Andria and his family being what it was, we decided we would do anything within our power to help them. Parting with the seven hundred dollars did not leave us too much. The fact that we had any cash at all on hand was due to the collapse of the banks that claimed our entire savings. After that we had no faith in the banks.

Jovo left all money matters to me, so of course I would know the best place to hide our money. Milka was always told of the most current hiding place. She needed to know, if something should happen to us, but it must be a secret. Once she protested, asking what if she made a mistake and told someone.

Jovo sometimes chuckled when I came up with a new place to hide the money. "It would take a Czar's treasurer to find the money. Mara, you are so clever."

A few hiding places are still fresh in my mind, my child's as well. It was after the banks were in full operation, and we received a check for one hundred and twenty-one dollars—not all we lost, but it was a windfall to me. Yet the distrust of banks lingered on.

Milka slept in a big brass bed with big brass spheres atop tall pillars at each side of the headboard and footboard. Well, they were fastened in place by small screws, which I removed from one sphere on the footboard. There, on a long length of string, I suspended a wad of cash tightly wrapped in one of Jovo's socks. Replacing the sphere that evening, I revealed to Jovo and Milka my new hiding place.

Another brilliant place was in the ash box of our kitchen stove. That summer I decided to have the stove hooked up to gas—an expenditure I decided we could afford. Jovo couldn't stop laughing, saying that if I just happened to fire up the stove to bake something, our cash would turn to ash. He was right.

Another was in a glass jar of the dirt of the crawl space at one of our rental apartments. Some neighbor boys were chasing a cat that ran under the house. I nearly fainted from panic. Well, that choice was short lived.

In another apartment I managed to pry up a loose board in the closet floor.

Of course, the agreement to repay us was sealed with a handshake—nothing in writing. Milka was told in detail the importance of a promise. A promise guaranteed by one's word is a bond stronger than any words on paper. We felt that she should know about the loan and understand what goes on in the financial world. Our repayment was completed not just in money, but in lifelong friendship.

We did not, however, reveal one other very important aspect of our meeting with Andria and Alice. The worrisome subject of what would become of Milka if we both should die at the same time needed to be settled. I had always been so paranoid about such an event, realizing full well that we would have to make some kind of plan for her welfare and future. So that evening when we brought up our concern to our friends, their immediate response was such a comfort. They would take Milka into their family.

Some weeks later, on one of our visits to Andria's home, he jokingly asked Jovo and me if we would ever marry.

"Surely by now you have each passed the test." We looked at each other, Jovo hesitating to say anything. After all, it would be my decision, he knew that.

"Yes, yes. At least, I am ready," I happily said. "What about you, Jovo? Would you consider me after all this time?" I asked.

Jovo answered, "I have always hoped for this, but only if you feel you can give up your share of the pension."

You probably guessed it; I didn't go through with it until June 12, 1938. My child was fourteen years old then. Milka was shocked. She had assumed, I believed, that somewhere along the line we had married. A child's dream, I suppose. Needless to say she was overjoyed. I gave up my share of the pension. Can you believe that?

Soon after that we purchased a home and became a "real" family. And what a home it was. Many a Sunday I dragged Jovo and Milka to different parts of town by trolley in search of a home.

Soon Jovo became tired of the search, declaring, "When you find what you like, let me know."

We both knew that it would be my decision. What a find! Two stories. The upper floor was a rental apartment (bringing in a bonanza of thirty dollars monthly). Three bedrooms, a formal living room and a formal dining room with French doors separating them, and a crystal chandelier. The upper sash of the living room windows was centered with an emerald-green French symbol of the fleur-de-lis. We could easily assume that the former owners were French people.

The city of Detroit was settled with a great many French people. Detroit is a French word.

The kitchen was replete with tiled counters and glass-doored cabinets. There was a built-in ironing board and a full basement with a kitchen and bathroom. The bathroom had a large bathtub, a sink with a tiled counter, a laundry chute emptying into the basement, and tiled flooring and walls. The contrast to the outhouses of the past was amazing. We found ourselves just gazing at it, just for the reassurance that it was still there. All brick too. The price was four thousand three hundred dollars. Jovo was flabbergasted—speechless. We paid cash. I had hoarded it all, putting my pension money in as well. I commented that his hard work was a huge contribution.

He replied, "Any fool can make money; it takes a good woman to safeguard it." Cheecha became Papa, master of the house.

# Chapter 27

From the beginning of our lives together, I had one great, consuming concern. I had many such great concerns, but this one was of the greatest importance. My health, when I took spells of dizziness and fainting, worried me greatly. What would become of my child if I died? Would Jovo keep her and take care of her? As the years passed, I had assured myself with good reason that he would never abandon her. His attachment to her was too strong.

As I mentioned earlier, Milka would be absorbed into Andria's family should Jovo and I die simultaneously. But there was this big BUT. This was a big dilemma. I could not speak of it to Jovo. After a time of considering and looking for all sorts of solutions, I convinced myself I had found the perfect one. Of course, this was to be my secret.

On Sundays, weather permitting, after church I would suggest that we visit some friends I had made in church. He was an agreeable man, so the three of us would set out and make a day of it. Trolley transportation was time consuming. Because no one we knew had a phone and neither did we, these were acceptable surprise visits. I preselected families with sons; my quest was to find a suitable partner for my daughter. The fact that she was so young did not deter me one bit.

If the sons were a year or two older than my child, I lied, raising her age to match theirs. The same deception was used if they were younger. I remember vividly Milka's timid question about why I didn't tell her the truth about her age.

All I said was, "Remember, I told you a long time ago that someone had thrown you away, and I found you, and that I never really knew your age. "Yes, I had confused her with a hurtful, cruel, totally inexcusable lie. What compelled me to say such a thing, I can't say. I recalled at that moment when my child said that, that I had first uttered those cruel words when she was about four or five years old. All those years I had terrified her with a threat that since she was already a throwaway child, that I could do the same, and today could be the day.

In addition, to prove that she was not my child, I would hold her up to a mirror and say, "See, you are not mine. You don't look anything like me. Your hair is poor with a reddish color. You have freckles. Your eyes are not dark like mine, and your nostrils flare when you speak."

Whatever made me say that about her nose? Was that insanity or not? I deserve a flogging. Was I insane, and am I still? Now what occurs to me is that the circumstances in my own life of being given away by my mother had much to do with my behavior. Too late now to undo the past.

My intent was to find a suitable family with a son whom I would judge to be the one she would marry at the earliest time of her life, the law permitting, of course.

Jovo was not her father, and should I die, my child would be left in an unfavorable circumstance. I worried that her reputation would somehow be sullied, branding her unsuitable for anyone. Just recalling all of that makes me ashamed.

This search went on for years until Jovo put his foot down. He had known all along. I didn't exactly promise that I would stop; I kept my eye out every chance I got. But no more surprise visits to anyone's home.

My child frequently, sadly, asked why I did not have any pictures of her father. Well, they just were never taken, nor were there pictures of me. A photographer never found his way to our village. She constantly pressed me for an answer. .What did he look like? So, I dug into the past, coming up with a description that made her happy.

"He was of medium height, with brown hair, gray eyes, and a complexion a lot like mine," I said. Telling her any small detail about her father pleased her, but I dwelled too much on his ill treatment of me.

Once night I overheard her prayers. Mentioning her father, she wished him peace. Also, she prayed that God would take special care of her Cheecha.

"Please, God, don't take him away. And I pray he would not be mad at me if he knew that I pray for my father too."

Decades later I had reason to wonder about those differences. Could Beverly have been correct in her analysis of my mother's reason for sending me out of her life? Did I possess the genetic blueprint that transferred to my child, thereby making her physical appearance so different? How was I supposed to know about the anxiety, guilt, and confusion I was heaping on my child? My own fears that he would leave led me to blaming my child, should he do so.

"It will be your fault if your precious Cheecha leaves us. You are not of his flesh and blood, so he can forget about us easily." I frequently, angrily directed those deadly words at her.

Milka never reacted, which infuriated me. I felt she would indeed be his reason for abandoning us. Besides infuriating me, I was certain she was driving him crazy as well. She never let him out of her sight. Even before she could tell time, I saw her checking the clock. I would ask myself, *What does she know about time?* Of course, a child could and probably did know where the hands on the clock should be when he walked through the door. If he was late, she disappeared into her room, and a few times I saw her crawling under the bed to hide, I suppose. If he was late, I would quietly panic as well—this was the day.

Jovo was followed wherever he went. Out into the garage, the yard, or up in the attic. When we purchased our home, repairs and painting were necessary, as is to be expected. Milka was right behind him no matter whether he was up on the roof as he checked the shingles after a storm, or as he replaced a cracked windowpane, or whatever else he was engaged in repairing. Instead of sending her away, he constructed a little toolbox for her, filling it with smaller tools. She learned at his side to do all sorts of "boy" work, as I called it.

I told her she had the makings of a boy, and that as a girl she was not much. "Oh, Mara, Mara!" Where was my compassion and understanding of my child's suffering? Often I found myself resenting bitterly the advantages that she had, saying to myself, *Who is she that she should have such an easy life?* Life with me was hell; I regretfully became aware of that in my dotage.

# Chapter 28

*D*espite my matchmaking schemes, Milka had been slipping away from me. Her love of learning instilled by Jovo from her childhood was a big help. She excelled in writing stories based on Jovo's adventures when he immigrated to America in his early twenties. He told stories of the West and cowboys, all of which I felt was more appropriate for a boy. Milka spoke of college and becoming a teacher or a nurse.

What a waste of time. Marriage to a good provider would have served her better. Children, perhaps two, I decided, as though I was a wizard who could bring that all about.

Why was I so against Milka's enthusiasm? Jovo was the opposite, with encouragement and praise I could not understand. They were foolish dreamers, I decided.

A nagging discontent, deeply rooted in my village where survival was a daily goal, was ever present. At least I had a value; my work mattered. In America my life of city living denied me the joy of Mother Earth's magical ways found in fields, forests, streams, farm animals, and the bone-breaking fatigue that satisfied me.

I was slipping into despair, feeling that life had become predictably unsatisfying. A dark cloud hung over me. How could I have imagined or predicted that a greater black cloud would descend upon the world?

World War II was making its presence known through letters from my village. People I knew were fleeing to America. Immigration was strained as America became involved in the conflict. I felt a dread so profound that it was eroding my physical and mental health. Memories of the horror of World War I that I hoped would never repeat itself had taken over my life.

Overnight, it seemed, Japan attacked Pearl Harbor. The ensuing frenzy of building a "war machine" capable of protecting America took over our lives in a single-minded mantra "America must win the war."

Against my wishes Milka took a factory job that so exhausted her, it affected her health. A seven-day, ten-to-twelve-hour shift resulted in near baldness and twitching facial muscles. A shop nurse sent her to a YWCA camp to recover. She was there when Japan surrendered, having worked for three and a half years. The Young Woman's Christian Association is owed a great debt for their rescue of hundreds of female factory workers throughout America.

The damage to her health was slow in healing, but it was her new attitude to quickly disagree with my old rules. A confidence, plotting her future without confiding in me, rankled me. What kind of female had she become? She cried as she learned of her many neighboring friends, childhood friends, who perished in the war or worse yet, as she often lamented, those with wounds too severe to ever mend.

Her restlessness and a detachment from Jovo and me concerned us both till one day she announced that she had to get away from it all by going to Arizona. I was horrified. The shame of a properly raised Serbian girl doing such a thing meant only one thing: She was spoiled, if you know what I mean. Who knew how she conducted herself in the factory that I had already concluded led her to ruination? The year was 1947; Milka was still agonizing about the war.

Jovo would have strangled me if he could get away with it. I resented his attitude that Milka had a right to pursue her life. He felt that her escape was important to her recovery. She was certainly a casualty of the war, he reasoned.

Total madness consumed my mind as I concocted a story that Milka was pregnant. Surely she would not leave. She had to prove the rumor false. Right?

The rumor never reached her ears till years later I confessed my crime. Just a shrug of her shoulders, turning away without comment, left me judging her as weak.

Milka kept in touch with us, sending plenty of cards and letters. Five months in Arizona had restored her health and spirit. When she returned she quickly enrolled in a business school, finished her studies, and immediately thereafter took a fine job with a law firm.

We were a family again. Jovo was overjoyed, but he was visibly not in the best of health. Milka took note of the swollen legs and the look of pain in his face.

# Chapter 29

*I* was fuming that Jovo had gone to Saint Petersburg, Florida, following his physician's suggestion that he seek a warmer climate to ease the circulatory problems in his legs.

It was the dead of winter in 1949 in Detroit, blizzard after blizzard. And there he was, basking in the sunshine and warmth of the Gulf of Mexico waters. One evening at exactly ten o'clock, Jovo phoned, all pleased with himself, saying, "Well, Mara, I have great news. Sell the house and everything in it. I have purchased a furnished home here—we will be living in Florida."

Milka was there, looking at me in dismay, not having any idea of what I was hearing. I do not recall all the names I called him. Hanging up on him, I started a tirade probably heard by the neighbors. How dare he make such a drastic decision without consulting me? Florida! What did I care about that? Giving up my beautiful home was out of the question. Milka was enjoying my misery. She started to laugh.

"I congratulate Papa on finally taking the helm. You have never allowed him to make any decisions. Now he is asserting himself," she crowed.

I phoned Jovo right back, declaring most emphatically that I would not sell my home or move to Florida. He asked that I put Milka on the phone, explaining in a very cheerful voice that he preferred Florida and would come home only to settle his affairs. Milka repeated what he said.

"I am going to suggest to your mother that we sell the Detroit house and divide all of our assets, leaving both of us free to choose where we want to live."

"Yes, yes, yes" is all I heard coming out of Milka's mouth. Then, "That seems fair to me, and I will look forward to living in Florida. I'll tell Mama."

By then I could see that there was a conspiracy afoot, and I would have none of it till I heard Jovo's proposed terms. That really did it. What Jovo wanted was clear to me. He did not want to return. My daughter would join him, and I could do as I pleased with his blessing and my share of the money.

I suppose I should mention that the salt water of the Gulf of Mexico, as Jovo frequently walked through the surf, had healed the blood-engorged varicose veins in Jovo's legs. That and the sunshine invigorated him and actually added at least ten years to his life—I am positive of that

The veins had caused a great deal of discomfort, especially in the winter, and were aggravated by the long hours spent on his feet at his job. He was an all-purpose man; janitor, groundskeeper, and heating system maintenance specialist.

For many years the only relief for the bulging veins was the application of leeches. These were purchased at the drug store and carried home in paper cartons. Often Milka volunteered to walk the city block or two to get the leeches. The leeches reached the point of practically bursting with the "dead blood." Salt was sprinkled on them to force their release from the flesh of Jovo's legs.

No way would I allow the scattering our assets to the winds, as I saw it, so I bragged to friends and neighbors that we were moving to Florida, making it sound like my very own idea.

It was true, what Milka said. I had not allowed Jovo any decision making. Well, it was done now, so I had to live with it. As it turned out, Florida was pure heaven compared to Detroit. Of course, I would never admit that to those two.

He reveled in his new role. He made friends everywhere he went. I was always included by him, no matter what the occasion. I was looking at him with eyes opened for the first time since we commenced living together. His ideas and suggestions of selling the house he had purchased and selecting a site upon which to build a house we both would enjoy surprised me. Constantly I had to remind myself that any objections from me would just put me on thin ice. Of course, I went along, but privately I had moments of feeling betrayed by the two of them. Of course, I courted misery on a regular basis. Now I realize that I never gave up on making myself miserable, such a pro.

# Chapter 30

*S*urprise, surprise, my daughter got married. Just like that! I was eating a grapefruit in the kitchen by myself when she said, "Mama, I'm getting married in about a month."

*Why the rush?* I wondered...oh, never mind.

In surprise, then shock, "You?" I asked. "When did that happen?" I didn't even know she was going out with a man. "Okay, so who picked you? An American, I suppose." I was getting a little mad at her. Any mother would understand.

"Yes, an American. He is going to be a lawyer in about a year. There will be no wedding to plan. His parents and you and Papa will not be there either. His best man, Robert Goldrick, and my friend, Julia Medich—you know her—will stand up for me. We will leave right after the ceremony. Bob has to get to the Stetson University law school in DeLand, Florida, the next day."

So it happened at seven in the evening on Tuesday, February 8, 1951. They were married at the Bay Pines Veterans Affairs chapel here in Saint Petersburg.

My feelings that the American groom, Robert George Bamond, would not amount to much were changed pretty fast. He set up his own office on our main street, Central Avenue. As it turned out, his family was very well known. His father, Arthur, was a policeman.

I forgave her for not having us at the wedding. And I forgave her for the dinner I fixed for them that was a waste of time. So, I invited his parents to come for that same dinner the next day. It was very nice to meet them for the first time. I bragged to all my friends that my Milka had done well for herself—for a change. She was twenty-six years old. It was about time.

# Chapter 31

*J*ovo and I lived comfortably. I had my church group, and he had elected to join a different church and denomination. This gave him his own circle of friends. I was too tired to object. His newfound independence annoyed me, but I liked his friends, and I did like to spend time with them.

The world spins around in mysterious ways; Jovo and I were living in Florida, so were Milka, her husband, and their two children when I received a phone call. Guess who? Zeka! I had not had any contact with that woman in over thirty years. Well, well, well, Zeka was inviting herself and her cousin, Jela, to come visit us in Florida.

What possessed me I can't say, but I heard myself saying, "Oh, sure, Milka will pick you up at the train station and bring you to my house."

When I told Jovo, he just shook his head, saying, "What can it hurt?" By that time I had told him of the theft.

Milka and I met the women at the train station. Zeka had aged, I noted, but then, so had I. To tell you the truth, I felt absolutely no animosity toward Zeka. I really surprised myself. The women settled in. It was very pleasant. Milka took us here and there to show off Saint Petersburg. We had a fine time, and Zeka was genuinely charmed by Milka and her children. On the evening before their departure, Zeka became sad and weepy.

She said, "Mara, I sent Ilija's cousin Peter to rob you. I've regretted it, so I came here to confess."

I just looked at her, said nothing, and just went into the kitchen to fix some coffee, saying to myself, "Money would be better than a confession." There was no mention of restitution…oh well.

I missed a golden opportunity to thank Zeka for the train fare from West Virginia to Detroit. And even though I had repaid that loan, she deserved my thanks. Whatever her objective was, the end result brought us out of abject poverty and a life in a cellar with no future for my child. Milka would have been part of the same dismal dead-end existence as her parents. Zeka never heard any words of thanks or gratitude from me. The stolen money was irrelevant. She is gone now, so there went the opportunity and moral obligation to thank her for her grand gesture.

When Milka's youngest child was almost two years old, Jovo announced one day that he was seriously thinking about adopting Milka.

"What for? She's too old. Are you crazy?" I asked.

"No, I am not crazy. It has been on my mind for a very long time. I want to do it, but I have to ask Milka if she is agreeable. Why is it that I even tell you anything?" he scolded me angrily. "This is our business. Hers and mine. I am certain she will be happy when she hears what I have to say," he continued, looking quite pleased with himself.

*What do I care what they do?* I told myself. But I knew I was jealous. An attorney already known to us, James T. Russell, represented Jovo in his petition to adopt. Mr. Russell was amazed, saying he had never handled a case like that.

Stubborn as ever, I refused to go to the courtroom to witness this event. The judge was impressed. I heard later that he was very much impressed indeed. He asked Jovo why he wanted to adopt his stepdaughter at this point in her adult life.

"Well, your honor, when she was a child, I could not bring myself to impose my name upon her. She would not have understood. And also, she would not be able to make that choice at a young age. I have always considered her my own, so now I want to make her my legal heir," said Jovo.

There were handshakes all around, I heard, and the judge kept saying how proud he was to be on the bench that day.

Seems there was a reporter with the *Saint Petersburg Times* present in the courtroom. He considered the matter newsworthy. There was a small article in the newspaper a few days later. When I saw that, I felt foolish that I couldn't understand how much it mattered to the two of them.

That court date I had agreed to look after Milka's children. Upon arriving at our home, the way they carried on, one would think Milka had just become come a czar's daughter.

"My papa," she and the little ones sang and danced about. Jovo sat watching, singing along and clapping. The celebration continued. Papa was a fairytale czar, solidly enthroned that day.

Jovo passed away in his seventy-fifth year on July 16, 1958, after a brief illness. To the end a gentleman, a kind, considerate man admired by many and remembered by many more.

# Chapter 32

On my eightieth birthday, my daughter took us to a very unusual restaurant for dinner called the Kapok Tree Inn. It was just the two of us. I can't recall now why her family was not there. In my usual critical fashion, I began to make negative comments about the restaurant.

My criticism was, "You told me this place was special. I don't see anything here that is special. There are too many people. What's it going to cost? You always spend too much."

I'm sure I added a lot more, but I just don't want to remember. She was silent; she always was. No matter what I said, she was silent; she always was.

Suddenly she exploded, her face red. Speaking almost inaudibly her voice was fierce and angry. She really told me off. At first I could not believe what I saw, but the words, they were another matter.

"You," she said, eyes blazing, "have never accepted me as a daughter. From as far back as I can remember, you told me that

I was not your child. That some woman had discarded me along the railroad tracks, and that you too could discard me. And I suppose you don't remember holding me up in front of a mirror, telling me how ugly I was. 'Your hair is pathetic, you have freckles, your nostrils flare when you speak, and your eyes look slanted. Where in the world did you come from? Maybe you would've made a better-looking boy.' You said it and said it for years. Always pointing out little girls you said were prettier than I. Mean, mean, that was you then, and you are still mean and critical. I thank God for my Papa, Jovo. He loved me. I always could count on him to show kindness. He never tore me down."

At first I did not recall saying anything like that. It seemed to me like a lot of silly complaints and drama.

Milka continued on. "Furthermore, I am tired of hearing how Mrs. so-and-so has a daughter like you deserve. And in addition, Mrs. so-and-so's grandchildren were so wonderful. You wished they were yours. Who takes care of you? Who takes you to the doctor? Who takes you grocery shopping? Who takes you to visit your friends?

"Since Papa's passing you have spent at least two long weekends per month at our home. We take you along on picnics and other outings. Never appreciative or satisfied, you complain about foolish things, like too much sand—it gets into your shoes, too much sun as well, too many people, too long in an auto, the wrong kind of food I brought."

"From this day forward, I am not your daughter nor are you my mother. I will continue to do all I have done in the past, but I am shutting you out of my life. I am writing you off. It feels good."

With that, she snatched up her purse, pulled out my chair, took my elbow, and forcefully propelled me out the door. Quite frankly, nothing of what she accused me of registered in my mind. Clearly she was crazy, like her father. We left our meal untouched.

Silently she drove me home, took me to the door, unlocked it, and left me standing there. Did I need any more convincing that she was neurotic? Some days passed when I realized that I missed her daily early morning phone calls. She always checked on me. I freely admit that the silly episode in the restaurant did not trigger any remorse or regrets on my part. After all, I had done nothing wrong. She was exaggerating.

Milka had not lied to me. She continued to care for me. She still continued to take me shopping, to keep appointments, and to visit my friends. Months later as she was driving me to my home following the usual trip to the grocery store, I reached over and placed my hand on her knee. Her reaction nearly caused a wreck as she jerked her leg away. The car lurched sideways, and for a moment I was frightened.

"Don't touch me!" she screamed. "What do you want from me? It's too late, do you hear? I don't feel anything for you anymore."

Good God. This was what I got when all I wanted to do was pat her a little. That night, sitting in my darkened living room, I found myself questioning myself. Was it possible that I had been inadequate as a mother? Surely my comments about my friends' daughters and their children were only meant to help her shape up. What was so wrong about that? After all, she was not as talented as I had expected her to be. Mentally I went through a list of ways she could have improved her housekeeping, cooking, and such. Wasn't it my job to prod her on? To help her? Of course it was. Slowly I became aware of the long passage of time as I was sitting there in the dark. My mind began to focus on my childhood, my life in Europe—my miserable existence.

Why had I been so unaccepting of my child? She was really a sweet, obedient, practically invisible child. No trouble at all. Yet this child must have wanted and needed more. My strictness, my watchfulness, protected her. Of course it did. No harm would come to her, as I could see trouble ahead at every turn. Limiting her life to school and a playmate or two lessened the opportunity for bad people to do her harm. Still she was not appreciative of my duty to keep her safe. I did say some awful things. How she could not understand my inability to forget or forgive, or how I indulged her, how her stepfather coddled her, how she did not show gratitude. In short, she got too much, deserving none of it. Yes, she had too much. Besides, she had an easy, lazy life. School was a means of getting away from me. The system plotted this scheme to control children, to fill their lives with information that would corrupt them, pulling them away from family. So what did she do that was useful while not in school? Washing a few dishes and scrubbing the kitchen and porch floors were exactly tailored to children's work. The floors were unpainted and easily stained, so suds and bleach restored them to near whiteness. She was learning to wash clothes, ironing properly, and mending socks. No toiling in the fields or gathering of wood for her.

She read constantly, bringing home so many books from the library, till they consumed too much of her time. I could read by then, but only the Bible. Such foolishness—often I threw away magazines Jovo brought home. She would get upset, but I only saw it as damaged. But why did I so enjoy passing it on? This revelation was so late in coming. Only God could hear my prayer for forgiveness. Finally, I was absorbing the often-heard and scoffed at word: love. Yes, love. An emotion I had never become acquainted with—and did not want to. Love, to me, was an empty word.

I now recall an incident that occurred in Milka's kitchen as I was spending a few days at her home. She was stirring the makings of something for dinner, and at the same time holding her youngest child, still an infant, with her left arm.

I don't know what came over me, but I felt some kind of emotion I cannot define. I went and stood at her side and asked, "Would you tell me what it is that you feel for your children, that you call love."

Milka, without hesitation, replied, "All I know is that I would give my life for any one of them," and just kept on tending to that pot.

Pain, the likes of which I had never felt before, brought on such a surge of tears. I had to quickly turn away and leave the room.

Years later I actually overheard my daughter telling her dear friend, April, what had happened that day, and how sad it made her feel.

Milka gave birth to four children in a period of ten years. Laura, George, Fay, and finally Phillip. She was thirty-eight years of age then. Lord, oh Lord!

After the birth of her second child, I admonished her to simply stop now. So, when Fay—number three—was born, I was so mortified, yes, mortified. And what's more, the shame that all she could do was breed children. Well, I informed her that too much was too much, and that I was humiliated whenever I went to church, and especially on meeting days of our Serbian Sisters of the Church. I raved on and on about Milka being a breeding cow. Can you believe that? What must those women have thought of me, especially since some of them were mothers of multiple children? I swear my attitudes were so bizarre. God help me. My grief was overwhelming. I had destroyed so much. My daughter became concerned when she noticed the malaise in me.

One day she asked, "Are you taking your medications? Are you eating enough?"

She even took my temperature and listened to my heart as she put her ear to my chest. I longed to stroke her hair, thinking of all the years when she was a little girl as I combed her hair and wrapped it in rag strips to curl it, never pausing to lovingly pat her on the head. Honestly, I did not take any notice of my declining state of health. Sadness filled my days. At the end of that month

I was hospitalized. The diagnosis was not too conclusive, but I had become dehydrated.

After spending a week in the hospital, I was released to my daughter. I was set up in one of the children's rooms.

My daughter took care of me the way a mother cares for a small child. She gave me sponge baths, fed me, and walked me to the bathroom when I was finally strong enough to graduate from the bedpan routine. Her manner as she combed my hair was soft and caring, speaking to me in a before-unheard tone. I guess I was hearing her for the first time. From time to time, while in my weakest state, I felt a letting down of my guard. Then as I regained my strength, I began to pull away. There was a conflict raging inside of me that I did not understand. Why was I so hell-bent on reverting to my old ways? Why could I not just accept my child's overtures of kindness? Why was I fearing the loss of something I could not put a name on?

A visit to the doctor for a final check-up, with his pronouncement that I could go home, did not exactly please me. Admittedly, the attention I was getting was spoiling me. Doctor Arnold questioned me about this, and that annoyed me enough to assume an attitude of belligerence.

"What do you want with all the questions? I'll go to my house when I choose to."

"Frankly, Mrs. Djakovich, if you were my mother, I would get you a one-way ticket to Yugoslavia," the doctor said.

I thought he was joking. Some joke. Yet he had managed to get under my skin.

My daughter had left the examining room to take care of the charges and paperwork. When I finished dressing, I prepared to leave the room, picking up my purse and sweater.

As I opened the door, I heard Dr. Arnold saying to my daughter, "Take her home today, or you will be my next patient."

"My goodness, how do I get her to agree? She is well now, very feisty and getting on our nerves."

Doctor Arnold's surprising reply: "Hey, it's easy. Just insult her."

I'd show them. Insult me indeed; it wouldn't work. Once in the car, I had a sudden idea.

"Let's stop at my house. There is probably some stuff in the refrigerator, rotting by now. Of course, if you had checked on the place..." What was wrong with me, anyway? No one needed to insult me. Not if I could beat them to the punch.

As we continued on our way to Milka's house, I said to her, "I've decided that I need to collect my belongings and my medication and go home. We can stop at the grocery store to pick up some things."

When we were back at the house, I announced to the family that I was going home. I don't know what I expected, but my statement fell flat. I guess that told me quite a bit.

# Chapter 33

All the good feelings that grew during my recovery seemed soon to dissipate. Business as usual, you could say. Yet there was something that lingered; something had taken hold. Gratitude began to replace my standoffish ways. Happiness, something I never allowed myself, played games with my mind. It was a hide-and-seek thing. Did I really understand it? Was it real? Did people really care that much? Did so simple a word as love have such power?

Reading the Bible daily was my routine. Finding comfort in it, I also learned that the teachings therein demanded something of me. The word forgiveness gnawed at me. How was it possible to forgive? Surely God did not expect us to cast aside the hurts holding the perpetrators blameless. Was there something I was not understanding? Quite often, in reading some passage on that subject, I would abruptly close the Bible. I could shut out anything I did not want to confront.

The Lord's Prayer really disturbed me. Reciting it at church with all those other voices really began to unravel me. *This Bible is so demanding,* I complained to myself. Then one day, upon awakening, I was determined to read the prayer, pondering each word. I was driven, I tell you; I was looking for a deeper meaning to my life.

"And forgive us our trespasses as we forgive those who trespass against us." The revelation was sudden and very clear—so simple.

If I could not and would not forgive, could I expect God to forgive me? Such a joyfulness enveloped me. My heart was lightened, my mind cleared, till it dawned on me that I was the only human who could forgive me. The fortress with which I had surrounded myself was now full of holes. My resolve was strengthened with daily readings from the Bible.

My family sensed a change in me. We never spoke of it. I was afraid I would sound pompous or even insincere. It was my secret mission as I struggled to win over my daughter. My prayers that she would understand and forgive me were fervent. I can't say what went on in her heart and mind. I never had the courage to ask. Mainly I was afraid of myself. Was I really strong enough to not backslide into my old ways?

Having been written off as a mother, at first I thought of it as a silly notion. She would get over it, of course. Before long, unexpected remorse was becoming my constant companion. In my dreams, oh, what disturbing dreams, memories materialized. It was as though I was watching myself on television. With persistent repetition my pesky daughter chastised me; her finger pointing at me at close range to my face was very unnerving. Bedtime had become an unhappy prospect as I tried to think of ways to shut her off. Sometimes I wondered if this was how God did it as we stood at the pearly gates, hoping for admission. I was really jolted one evening, when I realized that Jovo, too, was an unresolved matter that I needed to clarify in my mind. Did I really marry Jovo for what he could do for us? The respect I always had for him surely was sufficient, a payback, was it not?

One day when Milka had come to my home to do some house cleaning I was talking out loud to myself and of course you know who overheard me. God, you would think I had murdered that man. He had died peacefully after a brief illness at home. I had cared for him.

All I said was, "Peter Janovich was the kind of man I deserved: an astute businessman. His supermarket could have been even more successful with me at his side. His wife is lazy. Staying at home like some grand dama."

Her face and voice were so menacing it shocked me. The words so loudly hurled at me were hurting my ears—not the volume; it was the disgust-filled tone.

"How dare you insult him in his grave? My Papa was too good for you. He provided for us, very well at that. Look about you. What do you see? A nice home, paid for, money in the bank, and a pension too. Do you realize that his bones provide for you from his grave? What do you think the pension is all about?" She raved on and on when later this same episode came to me in a dream. I heard the meaning of the words for the first time.

# Chapter 34

Another reoccurring dream, which I happened to place no importance on, persisted in pushing itself into the present. "Oh, sure, I should have anticipated the lectures, the accusations. Spare me, Jesus," I pleaded one night as I prepared for bed. "She is like a raging river. Maybe I'm supposed to be swept away by it. Is this what old age is all about? The accursed children turning on us? Such a curse, such a curse. If only I had not given birth to her."

Jovo haunted me in my dreams, as I could see again his complete devotion to the child. I even recalled telling him to not take her to the hardware store, where a girl should not be seen because it would encourage her to do men's work. Jovo, in reply, had smiled and said, "Of course, Mara. You overlook one important thing here. It is good for our child to learn as much as she can about everything. Besides, her goodness and her smile will never be mistaken for anything but a femininity that will endure even with a hammer in her hand."

These dreams renewed recollections of many incidents when all I could think of doing was to criticize everything that Jovo did for the child. I had also accused him of doing all these things just to upset me.

Throughout my early life and continuing into my old age, I suffered from terrible headaches and fainting spells. Jovo had cared for me tenderly, applying cold cloths to my forehead and neck. Massaging my shoulders helped immensely. He had done the cooking when he returned from his job. On these occasions he solicited Milka's help. Lord, he was so completely taken in by her. Later they would walk to a neighborhood park, stopping off to buy ice cream cones. He would bring a small carton of ice cream for me. Instead of appreciating all that he did, I saw it as something he wanted to do to impress the child. I resented everything about her. Now I recognize the insidious jealousy that ruined my life and theirs.

I always watched him like a hawk. That, I can't be faulted for. Too many mothers overlook the opportunities that could present themselves rendering their female children vulnerable—you know what I mean? Knowing the nature of the male, a mother cannot be too careful; I know firsthand. I was not protected or warned. I figured it out myself at an early age, the male by nature's decree is a predator, be it father, son, uncle, brother, grandfather, family friend, neighbor, or teacher. A male is a male—not to be trusted when it comes to safeguarding a female. Jovo was possessed of high moral standards. He knew how to conduct himself as a stepfather to a female child.

The dreams were persistent. I sought more and more answers in the Bible. I can't say exactly at what point I had an awakening, so clear was the solution yet till that one moment I had not realized what I needed to do.

A phone call to Milka, a simple call where all I had to say was that I needed to see her as soon as she could conveniently come to my home. Without hesitation she assured me that she would see me within the hour.

"Mama?" she asked. "What is wrong? You look so tired. Are you not sleeping well? What about your medications? Are you taking them? I know you have a good supply."

"Yes, yes. I am taking my pills, but they cannot cure my illness. The problem is in my mind, my heart, and soul."

"Let's sit down, Mama." My child very solicitously led me to the sofa.

Putting her arm around me, she began to cry. "What's wrong, Mama? Please tell me. You frighten me."

My voice was gone. I could not utter a word as I began to let myself fall into her embrace, holding on tightly.

Dead silence. Neither of us spoke. The crying had ceased. *Now what?* I was asking myself. I was on the verge of something, and I had to sort it out. Number one, I had to cleanse my soul. I needed to confess my feelings of regret, to ask for forgiveness, but on the other hand it felt unnatural. Plus, I feared it would turn me into a weak person.

"God help me!" I screamed aloud. Jumping up, freeing myself from our embrace, I started. Words poured out of me. Regret after regret. One recollection after another as they crowded my mind. I don't remember most of it; weakness had taken over. I felt faint. Milka saw it, easing me down on the sofa and comforting me.

"Don't say another word, Mama. It's okay, it's okay," she said.

My mind wouldn't shut down. I would pause briefly, rest, then more regrettable memories of words said and deeds done would surface. Finally—I don't know when it was; it was more like the passage of two days, but my child reassured me that in reality we had talked for about two hours only—calmness came over me. Her face told me all I needed to know: She loved me. And not once did she have to say the words, "I forgive you." She kept reassuring me that everything was okay and that she understood and that there was nothing further for me to grieve about. I felt peace about facing God. My life was good.

The dreams that had plagued me in the time preceding my call for help were fading away. Milka gave me the reassurance I needed.

"It's in the past, Mama. Today is a new day."

Visits to Milka's home were different after that. With only Phillip, my youngest grandchild, still at home, it was somewhat empty in that regard, but my child and I spent more time together. My strength had returned. I was back to socializing with my church sisters. My daughter and I went shopping and visiting friends. Life was good. Besides, my child was calling me Mama. We were okay with each other. Praise God.

Milka had even shared with me that she had been chronicling the events of my life through the stories I had shared with her about my past and about the life she shared with me and Jovo. She wanted to tell my story. This pleased me.

My eighty-third year of life was soon approaching. My health was holding out. So was my mind. For that, I was really grateful. Enjoying my daughter and her family was enriching—a real panacea for all the old hurts, regrets, and self-recriminations. A clean slate had been handed me by God. My faith in Him was so profound. "Seek and you shall receive" was evident in my life.

*Mara Djokovich passed away in her sleep on*
*October 17, 1977, leaving us a memorable legacy:*
*"the essence of true womanhood."*

*The End*

# Epilogue

For decades, I entertained the idea of writing about my mother's life. Originally it was to be a brief history, written to better acquaint my children with their grandmother. In the beginning I wrote about her early years, then I would set my notes aside just to pick them up at some later date. As my writing progressed to the years of her adulthood, the hardships that she lived through, the direction the story was taking had changed. I was not only writing about my mother but all the people not even named in the story but who were beginning to become key players as well. That set the tone for my continued writing.

What I became aware of was that the story was also about the villagers—their customs, trials, and tribulations as a whole. Further, I was writing about their constant fight for survival in a difficult time and place.

Moreover, the strength of the women became a major focal point. Those were the women of that era anywhere in the world who were indeed the glue that held their families together and that held their communities together.

My own mother's toughness, born of difficult circumstances, demanded strength, both physical and mental, to meet each day head-on, accepting their roles as warriors, if you will, winning daily survival battles.

And so it was that long after the days of Mrs. Pekich and Mrs. Nadich, my continued quest to learn more throughout my mother's life impacted me so profoundly on my own life and who I became.

I have attempted to write in Mara's style of speaking and expressing herself.

Everything I have written of my conversations with my mother have been translated from Serbo-Croatian to English. Often, very often, I needed to refer to a dictionary belonging to Jovo Djakovich, my adopted father, for more accurate translations. The dictionary was printed in English-Croatian and in Croatian-English, authored by F.A. Bogadek in 1926.

Readers, I hope Mara's story will inspire you to research your origins, or at least read some books on immigration.

Our nation would never have reached the pinnacles of might and wealth had it not been for our immigrants from all parts of the world. The beginnings of our industrialization were borne on the shoulders of the immigrants and continue to this day, by the thousands, daily take the place of those who came before them, be it in the field gathering crops or operating oil rigs or working in factories or conducting scientific research or developing sophisticated technologies, etc. We all have our places, and our contributions are great.

Jovo Djakovich's greatest gift to my mother and myself was education. He planted the seed that grew within me to respect schooling and its benefits. I lived in ethnic communities in Detroit, Michigan, until we moved to Florida when I was an adult. In those communities I was surrounded by many different families of different European origins. I noted at an early age that parents, many of whom spoke little or no English at all, were still putting a strong emphasis on their children's learning English and doing their best in school.

Neighbors depended on each other to help in understanding what their children were learning in school. I saw a great deal more support for schooling than unfortunately I see today and, that is even among our educated citizenry.

Today's immigrants from European countries are more educated than the immigrants of yesteryear, and their children easily assimilate into our school systems and society. Case in point: my grandson Andrew graduated, with honors, I might add, from a high school in Saint Petersburg, Florida, in 2006. I will not name the student, a girl, who immigrated to America from Bosnia just a few years ago. She addressed the assembled teachers, parents, and students, first in flawless English, without a trace of accent, followed by a translation in Serbian. She was valedictorian. What does that say about the new immigrant? The opportunities are here, and they grasp their value, just as those who preceded them.

Jovo and Mara became naturalized American citizens. He in 1937, and she in 1938. When Jovo spoke of the importance of such allegiance to the new country, Mara understood immediately, saying it was easy to let go of her birth country. After all, what had it done for her?

The peasantry in her country was overlooked and taken advantage of—no match for what America had already gifted her with.

Writing, rewriting, and organizing all the material has taken decades. Finally, I believed that I had done a decent job of it. That is, till just about a few minutes ago. I experienced such a wave of sorrow, crying tears of shame.

The death of my poor Ilija, my father of whom I wrote in such derogatory terms, never phased me one bit till just now. The circumstances of his death did stir a deep feeling of sadness whenever I heard or read about a mining accident. But it is the circumstances of my birth that have finally, deeply affected me, forcing me to look at the reality of that fateful night in the cellar and the outcome; if not for Ilija there would be no me.

Finally, I have a connection to my father. I am overwhelmed. I pray that sharing my feelings with you will let Ilija know, wherever he may be, that I do honor him as my father.

This memorable awakening occurred at eight o'clock in the evening on Tuesday, January 23, 2007.

Writing Mara's story would not have been possible if not for the unbelievable change that had so dramatically come about, altering the course of her life and mine.

Without that change, all I would have accomplished was to create an exposé that served no purpose. Without her transformation, so clearly God ordained, all I would have done was to condemn her for her actions and attitudes that were forced upon her by the circumstances of her environment and experiences.

Made in the USA
Columbia, SC
21 September 2022

67306941R00143